T0277231

PORTUGAL'S ROTA VICENTINA

PORTUGAL'S ROTA VICENTINA

THE HISTORICAL WAY AND FISHERMEN'S TRAIL
by Gillian Price

JUNIPER HOUSE, MURLEY MOSS,
OXENHOLME ROAD, KENDAL, CUMBRIA LA9 7RL
www.cicerone.co.uk

© Gillian Price 2022
Second edition 2022
ISBN: 978 1 78631 143 6
Reprinted 2024 (with updates)
First edition 2019
Printed in Czechia on behalf of Latitude Press Ltd on responsibly sourced paper.
All photographs are by the author unless otherwise stated.
A catalogue record for this book is available from the British Library.

Route mapping by Lovell Johns www.lovelljohns.com
Contains OpenStreetMap.org data © OpenStreetMap
contributors, CC-BY-SA. NASA relief data courtesy of ESRI

Acknowledgements

Obrigada to Fabrizio for first mentioning the delights of Portugal. Laura joined Nick and I on the trail, José checked my language and definitely neither last nor least, Cicerone said yes! I am also grateful to the walkers who let me know details of changed route conditions, Liz Kantor and Les Lang in particular.

Updates to this Guide

While every effort is made by our authors to ensure the accuracy of guidebooks as they go to print, changes can occur during the lifetime of an edition. Any updates that we know of for this guide will be on the Cicerone website (www.cicerone.co.uk/1143/updates), so please check before planning your trip. We also advise that you check information about such things as transport, accommodation and shops locally. Even rights of way can be altered over time.

The route maps in this guide are derived from publicly available data, databases and crowd-sourced data. As such they have not been through the detailed checking procedures that would generally be applied to a published map from an official mapping agency, although naturally we have reviewed them closely in the light of local knowledge as part of the preparation of this guide. We are always grateful for information about any discrepancies between a guidebook and the facts on the ground, sent by email to updates@cicerone.co.uk.

Register your book: to sign up to receive free updates, special offers and GPX files where available, create a Cicerone account and register your purchase via the 'My Account' tab at www.cicerone.co.uk.

Front cover: Looking back over beautiful Praia do Malhão (Stage 4)

CONTENTS

Walkers on the marvellous Brejo Largo beach (Stage 5)

The Rota Vicentina Association

What makes the Rota Vicentina much more than sun and walking with stunning views over the ocean?

The Rota Vicentina is the result of the work of the private non-profit Rota Vicentina Association, that started close to 10 years ago. It's unusual to see a group of local family-run companies organising such a public-use project, but they started it from scratch, choosing the trails, marking them, organising information and promotion. Sustainability of such a special coastal area is a principal aim of the project, which is based on working cooperation between the local community and visitors.

The Rota Vicentina Association would like to share these recommendations with readers:

- Choose the shoulder and low seasons; in this way you'll help spread the tourist impact and will have a better holiday with fewer people and cooler temperatures

- Distribute your stay between the coast and the inland route options; this will ensure you enjoy a more diverse experience and less crowded conditions

- Check the options for complementing your self guided walk with some local services such as guided tours and cultural events or a group experience through the options available for booking on the Rota Vicentina website; you'll be supporting local identity and be enriched with a more authentic experience

- Choose local providers who are partners of Rota Vicentina and are aligned with the project, investing in the quality of your walking experience. In this way you'll be supporting the Rota Vicentina Association and will enjoy a more personalised service.

- Search out products that are local and sustainably produced, ask your providers before ordering or buying; you'll be supporting the beautiful rural landscape maintained by the local community and you'll be surprised by the quality

- Send the Rota Vicentina Association your feedback with comments and suggestions for improvement

The Rota Vicentina Association invites everyone to commit to a better world and way of travelling under the guidance of a local organisation that is focused on improving the relationship between hosts and guests, and supporting awareness while providing high quality products, services and facilities based on the local people, identity, resources and strategy.

Useful Links:
- The Rota Vicentina website rotavicentina.com
- The Rota Vicentina Blog, Blog.rotavicentina.com
- Semana ID, a special week in early spring with dozens of events and activities id.rotavicentina.com

ROUTE SUMMARY TABLE

Stage	Title	Distance	Ascent/Descent	Grade	Time	Page
Stage 1	Santiago do Cacém to Moinhos do Paneiro	21km	280m/315m	1–2	5hr 10min	34
Stage 2	Moinhos do Paneiro to Cercal do Alentejo	20km	160m/215m	1	4hr 30min	38
Stage 3	Cercal do Alentejo to Porto Covo	16.5km	185m/290m	1	4hr 15min	41
Stage 4	Porto Covo to Vila Nova de Milfontes	20km	160m/160m	1	5hr 15min	45
Stage 5	Vila Nova de Milfontes to Almograve	15km	130m/150m	1–2	4hr 30min	51
Stage 6	Almograve to Zambujeira do Mar	22km	110m/100m	1–2	6hr	55
Stage 7	Zambujeira do Mar to Odeceixe	18km	280m/310m	2	5hr	59
Stage 8	Odeceixe to Aljezur	19km	100m/100m	1–2	5hr 15min	63
Stage 9	Aljezur to Arrifana	12km	170m/160m	1	3hr	67
Stage 10	Arrifana to Carrapateira	24km	390m/480m	2	6hr	71
Stage 11	Carrapateira to Vila do Bispo	22km	290m/220m	2	5hr 10min	75
Stage 12	Vila do Bispo to Cabo de São Vicente	14km	80m/90m	1–2	3hr 30min	80
Total		**223.5km**			**57hr 35min**	
Inland route						
Stage 1IR	Odeceixe to São Teotónio	17km	350m/200m	2	4hr 30min	86
Stage 2IR	São Teotónio to Odemira	19km	150m/300m	1	5hr	90
Stage 3IR	Odemira to São Luís	25km	410m/250m	2	6hr 30min	94
Stage 4IR	São Luís to Cercal do Alentejo	20km	410m/400m	2	5hr	98

The marvellous rugged Vicentina coast (Stage 4)

INTRODUCTION

Looking back over beautiful Praia do Malhão (Stage 4)

If you have a penchant for dramatic cliffs and awesome ocean scenery with secluded sandy bays, are fascinated by gangly storks nesting on sea stacks, are able to walk around 20km per day, appreciate fresh fish and charming guesthouses and hostels... without forgetting ancient oak forests, brilliant carpets of wildflowers, sweet oranges, mouthwatering traditional Portuguese cuisine and inimitable custard tarts, then the Rota Vicentina is definitely for you. And rest assured it will quickly become one of your favourite treks.

Following the wild southwestern Atlantic coast of Portugal, this beautiful route inaugurated in 2012 is relatively little-visited but is on the way to becoming popular with walkers.

THE ROTA VICENTINA

Starting well to the south of Lisbon, the long-distance Rota Vicentina links the rural town of Santiago do Cacém with Cabo de São Vicente, the southwesternmost extremity of Portugal that juts out into the vast Atlantic Ocean, the last bit of dry land Portuguese explorers saw as they sailed forth into the 'great unknown'. The cape gave its name to the splendid rugged Costa Vicentina, and of course to the trek itself.

The route traverses two beautiful and fascinating regions of southern Portugal, the Alentejo and the Algarve. The first derives from 'beyond the Tejo', a reference to the river that runs through Lisbon. The Alentejo is reputedly the least developed of Portugal which for visitors translates as excellent walking country, a feature it has in common with the Algarve which owes its name to the Arabic Al-Gharb for 'the west'. This southernmost part of Portugal was under Moorish occupation in the 8–13th centuries until it was reconquered by Christian forces.

Nowadays it is well known as a retreat for sun-starved northern Europeans as it boasts 300 clear days a year! Both of these regions offer walkers a remarkable range of landscapes and habitats, from rolling hills to splendid wooded river valleys then olive groves and cultivated fields which back the exciting Atlantic coast, where marvellous breakers roll in and white-blue painted fishing villages cluster at the mouth of navigable rivers.

Myriad extra interest comes along the Rota Vicentina in the shape of local Portuguese traditions – such as feasting on goose barnacles – and history – in the shape of Arab-era castles and the Age of Discovery sites from the 1400s. Prince Henry the Navigator founded a navigation

A stunning beach awaits at Carrapateira (Stage 10)

Old adobe farmhouses in the interior testify to rural life

school near Cabo de São Vicente and famous Portuguese explorers the ilk of Vasco da Gama were in attendance.

The **Rota Vicentina** consists of two marked routes: the Caminho Histórico or the **Historical Way** and the Trilho dos Pescadores or the **Fishermen's Trail**. The former links Santiago do Cacém on an inland route over rolling hills to Odeceixe before moving closer to the coast the rest of the way south to Cabo de São Vicente. The shorter Fishermen's Trail mostly sticks to breathtaking clifftops from Porto Covo down as far as Odeceixe. There are dozens of variants. This guidebook uses a savvy combination with the best of both. The route described here, totalling 223.5km, begins at Santiago do Cacém, but not far along it veers out to the wonderful Atlantic coast before turning south to go the rest of

the way to Cabo de São Vicente in a total of 12 splendid day stages.

In addition, a four-stage inland route is described from Odeceixe running inland north back up to Santiago do Cacém to make an excellent 215km, 11-stage circuit for those seeking a loop rather than a linear walk. While these inland stages are less dramatic in terms of scenery, they give walkers an insight into life in rural Portugal. Many old houses constructed with clay, stones and stucco are still standing and used by farmers and herders, and small-scale agriculture continues to be a way of life. Alongside are eucalypt plantations and wide-scale logging.

Covering level ground for the most part, the Rota Vicentina is suitable for all fit walkers and has no technical difficulties. The walking follows a string of clear paths, lanes and country dirt roads with abundant waymarks and signposting. The odd steep section is included but overall it's easy to average walking. The sun is one factor to take into account as shade is at a premium and the wind should not be underestimated as this is the Atlantic coast and spending a day being battered can be tiring albeit exhilarating.

Thanks to the mild climate in this corner of Europe, the Rota Vicentina is feasible any time, year-round, with the sole exception of the midsummer months when it's just too hot. Each stage concludes in a hospitable village with excellent facilities and thanks to local transport, days can be varied and walkers can easily put together their own itineraries to suit individual holiday schedules.

PORTUGAL'S CLEAN ENERGY

The giant propellers of the Parque Eólico de Fonte dos Monteiros wind farm dwarf walkers (Stage 11)

The trek also touches on another small park located south, in the Algarve: the Parque Eólico de Fonte dos Monteiros is one of the country's many wind farms. Wind turbines currently cover 23% of domestic consumption, contributing to the country's clean energy campaign that makes use of hydro and solar power among others. In 2016 a whopping 58% of the power Portugal generated came from renewable sources, then amazingly in March 2018 the country produced even more than it needed and by 2040 it expects to be able to cover home demand completely with clean energy. Portugal is undeniably a world leader in this field.

A huge chunk of this trek is in the realms of the Parque Natural do Sudoeste Alentejano e Costa Vicentina where plant and bird life are protected. This encompasses the most extensive consolidated sand dunes in the whole of Portugal along with stunningly rugged headlands, eroded cliffs of coloured rock and wild beaches for swimmers and surfers alike. What's more, the park area guarantees that this beautiful coastline remains pristine. One of its great beauties is that it feels remote and you can walk for hours on end without meeting anyone. Even the villages and resort towns are low key and pretty quiet in low season – which is walking season. Naturally as summer approaches temperatures and prices rise as visitors pour in, but in any case it's too hot for walking then.

The Rota Vicentina is a very well thought-out sustainable walking route that is bringing visitors and income to coastal and rural areas of southwest Portugal. Over the last few years new accommodation and refreshment options have been springing up, to the advantage of all, walkers and residents alike. Go and do your bit.

HIGHLIGHTS AND SHORTER WALKS

The Atlantic coast sections of the Rota Vicentina are undeniably the most spectacular stretches of the trek, however an alternation of peaceful rural countryside contrasting with cliffs and beaches makes for an excellent combination. The complete trek means 12 stages but walkers with time limits can mix and match at will. A recommended nine-day loop visiting both coast and the interior is possible by starting out from Cercal do Alentejo and heading for Porto Covo then down the coast to Odeceixe (Stages 3–7). There you pick up the inland route (Stages 1IR–4IR) and follow it back to Cercal do Alentejo.

A suggested one-week stint is Porto Covo (Stage 4) as far as Carrapateira (Stage 10), otherwise in six days from Zambujeira do Mar (Stage 7) all the way to the trek end at Cabo de São Vicente (Stage 12). A short and sweet trip of just four days could start from Porto Covo (Stage 4) and head south to Odeceixe (Stage 7). These are just a couple of suggestions.

Walkers who are more comfortable with day walks will find plenty to get their teeth into on the Rota Vicentina. Nearly all of the villages visited during the trek can be reached by public bus, although a rental car gives more flexibility. You can always park at one of the stage starts, walk the route then catch a taxi back to where you began. Taxi services and other useful contacts can be found in Appendix B.

Lastly, the Rota Vicentina is continually being supplemented with interesting side trips. A handful are described in this guide as variants to the main route and lend themselves to circular day walks, namely at Arrifana and between Vila do Bispo and Cabo de São Vicente. See the Rota Vicentina website (http://en.rotavicentina.com) for more.

For a selection of day walks all over Portugal see the Cicerone guide *Walking in Portugal* (2018) by Andrew Mok and Simon Whitmarsh. Or, for day walks specifically in the Algarve region, see *Walking in the Algarve* by Jacint Mig and Nike Werstroh (Cicerone Press 2019).

WILDLIFE

Bird lovers will have a field day, especially on the Sagres peninsula where the trek ends. There, from the end of summer through autumn, massive flocks of migratory birds from all over Europe gather on their way south to the African continent to winter over. Buzzards, eagles, falcons, plovers, swifts, larks… a list as long as your arm.

A special treat on the Rota Vicentina are the white storks. These huge gangly birds construct cumbersome stick nests on power pylons across the countryside, however by far the most fascinating sites are along the clifftops overlooking the ocean. Here they prefer to nest on precarious sea stacks, out of reach of all but the voracious herring gulls who go for both eggs and fledglings – with little success as one of the parents is always in attendance. To feed, the storks fly inland to hunt for lizards, snakes, frogs

Storks build cumbersome nests right on the cliff edge

and fish in fields and wetlands. Until recently they all migrated south for winter but the discovery of easy food in landfill sites has meant large colonies are now year-round residents.

Inland rivers and streams are home to brightly coloured kingfishers, delightfully known in Portuguese as *guarda-rios*, river watcher. They share this habitat with otters and the attractive European pond turtle. Shy rabbits are commonly spotted skittering through wooded sand dunes but they need to be quick off the mark as they are the preferred meal of no fewer than 30 carnivores!

PLANTS AND FLOWERS

The glorious flora of Portugal is essentially Mediterranean in nature and the spring months (March through to June) are especially rewarding for wildflower enthusiasts. The coastal habitats along the Rota Vicentina route can be pretty harsh due to the strong winds, salt-saturated air and sandy soil but a surprising range of plants flourish and excel in keeping a low profile. Not far inland, woods and open fields host myriad blooms and trees.

The showy Hottentot fig (*Carpobrotus edulis*) is one of the seaside stars, forming dense carpets of pale yellow or bright magenta (*Carpobrotus acinaciformis*). Both have stocky fleshy truncated leaves and colonise sand dunes. Similar but more modest is the marvellously named ice plant (*Mesembryanthemum crystallinum*) with smaller feathery flowers surrounded by speckled leaves covered in glistening hairs, a bit like icing sugar. Another spreading champion that forms warm yellow domes along the coast is Spanish broom (*Genista hispanica*).

The rock rose or cistus shrub is widespread to say the least and comes in many varieties. The hardy bushes form impenetrable thickets and rush in to colonise land laid bare by logging. Gum cistus (*Cistus ladanifer*) is easily recognisable both for its sticky dark-green leaves scented with resin as well as its large showy white flowers which have a deep red splotch inside the petals.

Of the multitude of aromatic herbs, rosemary is a standout with robust low bushes loaded with tiny pale blue-lilac blooms in spring. Scented camomile is also common, a small daisy with minute white petals around a rich yellow heart. Pungent everlasting (*Helichrysum*) occupies sandy terrain with its silver woolly stems and yellow flowers.

Delightful delicate pale lilac iris-like Barbary nut (*Gynandriris sisyrinchium*) bloom fleetingly in woods, while the brilliant blue pimpernel (*Anagallis foemina*) prefers open fields. Lupins both yellow and blue are surprisingly common as are colourful snapdragons. Orchid lovers will recognise plenty of delightful specimens including the Ophrys insect varieties.

Clockwise from top left: yellow Hottentot fig; domed broom bushes; magenta Hottentot fig; Gum cistus; blue pimpernel; orange blossom

A couple of trees deserve a mention. Common in woodland is the strawberry tree (*Arbutus unedo*) with pretty creamy bell-shaped blooms and clusters of nutty red fruit used for both jam and brandy. Then there's the evergreen cork oak (*Quercus suber*) which forms veritable forests, a constant feature of southern Portugal. It has small dark-green leaves and acorns but more importantly very thick fissured elastic bark which is harvested every 6–10 years, exposing the blood-red trunk. Portugal supplies 50% of the world's cork.

Lastly, orange orchards emanate an unmistakable delicious perfume when their creamy white blossom appears.

Plenty of help in identifying plants and flowers in Portugal can be found at https://flora-on.pt as well as in the beautifully illustrated *Wild Flowers of the Mediterranean* by M Blamey and C Grey-Wilson.

GETTING TO PORTUGAL

The international airport on the outskirts of Portugal's capital Lisbon (www.lisbon-airport.com) is served by all the main European airlines as well as many transcontinental companies. Frequent train, bus and taxis provide links to the city where ongoing buses mean walkers can easily travel on to the trek start (see below).

On Portugal's south coast, Faro airport in the Algarve

Heading up through Santiago do Cacém at the trek start (Stage 1)

(www.faro-airport.com) is used mostly by low-cost companies. While it is rather too far from the start of the Rota Vicentina, it is handy for the trek conclusion, and is accessible by train, bus and of course taxi.

GETTING TO THE TREK START

The easiest way to reach the trek start, Santiago do Cacém, is on a Rede Expressos bus from Lisbon's Terminal Rodoviário at Sete Rios (this in turn can be reached from the airport by bus or metro – Jardim Zoológico stop). It's a 146km/2hr journey.

Chances are you'll have overnighted in Lisbon and got up at dawn to catch the early bus. A more relaxing option is to stay your first night in Santiago do Cacém to recuperate from the rigours of travel, then make an early start to the trek next day. See Stage 1 for facilities.

On the other hand should you opt to skip the trek's first three opening stages and head straight to the coast, catch the Rede Expressos bus from Sete Rios to Porto Covo; the 170km trip takes around 2hr 30min.

LOCAL TRANSPORT

Portugal has excellent reliable trains and a capillary network of buses; up-to-date timetables (*horários*) can be consulted on company websites. For the purpose of the Rota Vicentina, trains are only useful at the end (see below).

All of the villages and towns touched on during the trek – with the exception of Vale Seco/Moinhos do Paneiro in Stage 1 and Arrifana in Stage 9 – are served by bus, although if there's nothing handy a reasonably priced taxi can always be used (approximately €1/km). Details of local transport are given at the appropriate place during the route description. This spells alternative access/exit to fit in individual holiday requirements, bad weather or individual issues.

At the walk end, Cabo de São Vicente, a local bus connects to the village of Sagres where there's an ongoing run to Lagos and the railway line whence a link via Tunes through to both Lisbon and Faro.

For long-distance buses, seats should be reserved (at a ticket office or online), while for local runs you buy your ticket from the driver. Bus company logos are usually displayed at bus stops.

'Ticket' is *bilhete*, *ida* means 'single' whereas *ida e volta* (going and coming back) is 'return journey'. It's a good idea to learn the days of the week in Portuguese. Contact info for buses, trains and taxis is provided in Appendix B.

INFORMATION

A good general pool of information is available on www.visitportugal.com/en. Helpful tourist offices with multilingual staff can be found at many of the villages visited during the Rota

Vicentina – contact information is listed in Appendix B.

WHEN TO GO

Generally speaking, the September to June period is feasible for walking the Rota Vicentina. The spring months of March to May/early June then the late summer–autumn period of September to November are arguably the best times of year to walk the route. Despite cooling sea breezes, late June to August are generally stiflingly hot and not recommended as the route has a dearth of shade; the possibility of heat-stroke should not be underestimated. It is best to wait until the extreme heat of the summer has abated. A further advantage of not going in high beach-holiday season are the lower accommodation charges.

The midwinter months can be mild and quite superb albeit of course windy and chilly, although temperatures don't usually drop below 10°C at night. Rainfall tends to be heaviest December to January. Bottom line: don't be put off in the winter but do wrap up warmly and take reliable rain gear.

That said, whenever you go be prepared for extremes of weather which can do the whole spectrum in a single day – from scorching sun to strong winds and drenching rain.

ACCOMMODATION

An excellent range of high-standard *alojamento* (accommodation) for all budgets is available for walkers all the way along the Rota Vicentina. These start with the many hostels, some known as *pousada de juventude*. Always a good deal, these simple but inevitably well-equipped establishments usually offer dormitories with bunk beds and shared bathrooms although many also have comfortable double rooms with en suites. Use of a kitchen is included and meals are sometimes available too.

The next step 'up' are immaculately kept private rooms (*quartos*) known as *alojamento locale*, *residencial* or *hospedaria*, which may come with either an en suite or a shared bathroom; this will be reflected in the price. The choice continues through to mid-range hotels as well as boutique B&Bs in historic buildings. Just about everywhere provides wi-fi too these days, although most European walkers will enjoy the advantage of data and phone roaming.

It's best to book accommodation directly with the provider if possible (email or phone), although of course web agencies such as www.booking.com come in very handy. Preface calls to Portugal with the international code 351. Mobile phone numbers start with '9' and land lines with '2'. Advance reservation is only usually necessary at top-end places (which may be booked ahead by agencies for groups or self-guided clients) or around public holidays (see box).

Be aware that not all establishments accept credit cards so make

RESTAURANT & BAR

The lovely Youth Hostel at Arrifana (Stage 9)

PUBLIC HOLIDAYS

The main Portuguese public holidays are:
- 1 January (New Year)
- Good Friday and Easter Sunday
- 25 April (Liberation Day)
- 1 May (Labour Day)
- May/June (Corpus Christi)
- 10 June (Dia de Portugal)
- 15 August (Assumption)
- 5 October (Republic Day)
- 1 November (All Saints)
- 1 December (Independence Day)
- 8 December (Immaculate Conception)
- 25 December (Christmas)

sure you have a supply of euros cash just in case. All the villages and towns where the Rota Vicentina stages conclude have an ATM.

Camping is not allowed anywhere along the Fishermen's Trail of the Rota Vicentina and elsewhere is only permitted in designated camping grounds.

Suggestions for accommodation are given at the relevant stage ends in the route description as well as in alphabetical order in Appendix A. Many others can be found on the Rota Vicentina website and elsewhere on internet.

FOOD AND DRINK

A vast array of gastronomical delights awaits adventurous eaters along the Rota Vicentina, thanks to local traditions as well as the exotic spices and produce brought back by the seamen during the country's Age of Discovery. If your accommodation doesn't do breakfast (*pequeno-almoço*) then seek out the village coffee shop, *padaria* (bakery) or *pastelaria* (pastry shop) for hot drinks and toast or cakes.

Whatever the time of day or meal a luscious freshly baked *pastel de nata* Portuguese tart will go down well. A crunchy chewy pastry case is filled with egg custard and served warm with a dusting of cinnamon, a legacy from the country's spice trade. Quite frankly they deserve UNESCO World Heritage recognition.

For lunch, *sandes* are sandwiches, sold by most cafés and handy for picnics unless you prefer to make up your own from shop or supermarket items. As regards cheese or *queijo*, it's worth enquiring about flavoursome locally crafted

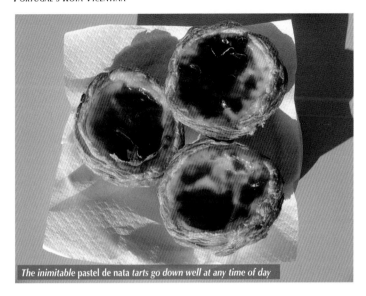

The inimitable pastel de nata *tarts go down well at any time of day*

varieties made with milk from *vaca* (cow) and more interestingly *ovelha* (sheep) and *cabra* (goat). These are best *fresco*, young, soft and spreadable whereas *curado* is mature, so the cheese will be firmer. Then there are cured pork sausages such as *chouriço* with garlic, wine and paprika. Another delicious lunch component is *presunto* (the Portuguese answer to Italian *prosciutto crudo*), courtesy of the black Iberian pigs which feed on acorns in the grasslands in the southwest. Another recommended taste experience advertised on café blackboard menus is a *bifana*, a warm roll filled with tasty fried pork. 'Please wrap it up' in Portuguese is *embrulhe por favor*.

As regards restaurant meals, *ementa do dia* is the day's menu. The Portuguese are the greatest consumers of fish in Europe and visitors can expect it sparkling-fresh on virtually every menu. *Peixe do dia* is the catch of the day and will usually be on display. *Dourada* is gilthead, *cavala* is mackerel, *marisco* shellfish, *camarão* prawns, *mexilhão* mussels, *lula* calamari, *polvo* octopus, *atum* is tuna, for a start. And you can hardly go wrong ordering *sardinhas* straight from the grill. One mouthwatering landmark dish is *feijoada choco e polvo*, a rich bean stew with cuttlefish and octopus.

However, the country's national dish is *bacalhau* – dried salted cod.

There are reputedly 365 different methods for preparing it, one for each day of the year! It all started off back in the 16th century when Portuguese fishing boats sailed to Newfoundland and discovered the immense schools there. Salting and sun drying the cod was a logical way to transport it. Until recently the fishermen would remain on the opposite shore of the Atlantic

Feijoada choco e polvo *is a delicious local speciality*

25

from April to October, however these days most of the cod is imported from Norway. Boiled, stewed, baked with potato, cheese and cream… it's a must-try.

Rice (*arroz*) is common on menus. Along with citrus and almonds it was introduced by the Moors as a crop in southern Portugal. Whenever on offer don't hesitate to order a *cataplana*, a round covered Arabic-style pan of rice stewed with fish or meat. Cooked slowly to retain the delicate flavours of the ingredients, it is a bit like paella and can be truly delicious.

Percebes are goose barnacles. The curious English name comes from an ancient belief that barnacle geese emerged from these crustaceans. Also known as 'Lucifer's fingers', the scaly cylinders are prised off the rocks at the intertidal zone by expert diving fishermen who dare the pounding waves of the Vicentine coast between January and August. Considered a great delicacy, they are boiled in water flavoured with herbs for the time it takes to say the Lord's Prayer according to the local usage. Watch how the Portuguese open and eat them. Another food challenge for the uninitiated are *caracóis* and *caracoletas* or snails, a springtime delicacy served in rural eateries with oil, garlic and herbs.

Meat or *carnes* is especially good in the Alentejo region where pork dominates. *Frango* is chicken, sometimes cooked with hot chilli.

Traders brought the potato (*batata*) to Portugal in the 17th century along with its sweet cousin *batata doce* which grows especially well in the southwest around Aljezur. With dark red-brown or purplish skin and yellow flesh, it is cooked up with octopus as well as made into desserts.

A short but fascinating note regards sweet oranges which are grown with great success in the Algarve. The fruit trees were brought from their native China to parts of Europe by Portuguese merchants in the 1500s and this orange is still known as a 'Portuguese' in languages as disparate as Romanian and Turkish.

On the *sobremesa* (dessert) front, trad restaurants always showcase their homemade delights. Keep an eye out for mouthwatering puddings or moist cakes made from figs, carob and orange, not to mention the enigmatic *baba de camelo* which translates as 'camel's drool'… but is a thick creamy concoction made with concentrated condensed milk. *Alcomonias* are sweetmeat lozenges of Arab origin containing honey, pine nuts and toasted flour.

Bom apetite! means 'enjoy your meal' and *muento bon!* means 'delicious!'.

It was the enthusiastic gourmet Romans who introduced grapes to Portugal and the country continues to produce excellent wines as well as the famous fortified port. Despite its name, *vinho verde* (green wine – as it's drunk young) from the country's northwest can be a dry white or even a red. The Alentejo region produces

An excellent range of Portuguese wines can be enjoyed

some excellent full-bodied wines of many varieties and plenty of drinkable refreshing rosé is available. One traditional liquor to look out for is fiery brandy *aguardente de medronho* made with the fruit of the strawberry tree. Last but not least, the tap water in Portugal is perfectly safe to drink.

À sua saúde – Cheers!

WHAT TO TAKE

What gear and clothes you take will depend on the time of year you choose to go, but the bottom line is – always much less than you think. There is no reason to load up your rucksack. Lightweight T-shirts, undies and socks can be rinsed out every day so you don't need to carry more than one change of basic clothing. Fatigue and diary writing will preclude reading of an evening so – apart from this guide – you won't need to carry books. Some suggestions follow for what to take:

• Medium-sized rucksack, 8–10kg maximum. Weigh it on your bathroom scales before leaving home, and don't forget to allow for water and food for the day.
• Water bottle
• Lightweight walking boots with good grip soles are recommended as they will help avoid twisted ankles and sore feet and are safer on wet slippery terrain

and loose stones. However, good-quality trainers with thick soles are also fine, although count on having to keep stopping on the sandy sections to empty them out. Sandals are only suitable for walking along the beach but it's much more enjoyable to go barefoot.

• Shorts as well as long trousers to protect legs from scratches on the occasional overgrown path
• Lightweight fleece
• Rain and windproof gear such as lightweight jacket, rucksack cover and over-trousers
• Snack food, easily replenished at village shops
• Whistle, headlamp or torch for attracting help in an emergency

• Trekking poles come in handy for transferring rucksack weight off knees and helping with balance when crossing streams.
• Sun protection is paramount – a wide-brimmed hat, high-factor sun cream and sunglasses
• Swimming costume and a lightweight towel (also handy for hostel stayers) come in handy when you want to stop for a swim. However, remember this is the Atlantic Ocean so beware strong currents and don't venture out too far.
• Basic first aid kit including electrolyte salts to compensate for excessive sweating

Note: walkers who prefer to do the trek without carrying a full

rucksack, just a lightweight day pack, can avail themselves of day-by-day luggage transfer services provided by local companies – see Appendix B.

WAYMARKING AND MAPS

The Rota Vicentina (RV) is pretty well marked and checked on a regular basis by volunteers. Waymarking for the Historical Way sections consists of adjoining red/white painted stripes, which are green/blue for the Fishermen's Trail. Where the way changes direction so do the stripes; whereas crossed stripes mean 'wrong way'. The markings are found on poles, rocks, tree trunks, buildings and fences. RV signposts supplement these with the addition of destination and distance.

As a general rule, unless the route description specifies otherwise, don't continue for more than a kilometre or so without seeing a waymark – should this happen, retrace your steps to the last one and hunt around.

Topographic maps (at a scale of 1:100,000) showing the route for the complete Rota Vicentina are provided in this book. A fairly clear 1:55,000 walking map on waterproof paper is produced by the Rota Vicentina organisation and available through their website.

Left: HW waymark telling you to turn right. Right: FT waymarks: top – this way, bottom – wrong way

DOS AND DON'TS

- Don't underestimate the Rota Vicentina – it's not a stroll along the beach but a multi-day trek that covers long distances. Find time to get in decent shape before setting out on your holiday. You will appreciate the wonderful scenery better if you're not overly tired and react better should an emergency arise.
- Don't set out late, even on a short stage. Always have extra time up your sleeve to allow for detours, wrong turns and time out.
- Keep to marked paths at all times and avoid trespassing on private property.
- Always close stock gates securely behind you – *fechar a porta*.
- Don't light fires.
- Be considerate when making a toilet stop. If you must use paper or tissues, carry it away. The small lightweight bags used by dog owners are perfect. There is absolutely no excuse for leaving unsightly toilet paper anywhere.
- After heavy rains expect to encounter waterlogged lanes and high stream levels. Take great care when fording them as there may be a strong current. Use trekking poles to check the water level, take off your boots and watch your step. If in doubt, choose the safer variants given.
- Carry food and plenty of drinking water as you won't find much en

route. Refreshment options are listed in stage headings.

- Don't forget sun protection – high-factor cream and a broad-brimmed hat. There's very little shade along the way.
- Don't rely on your mobile phone as there may not be any signal.
- Carry all rubbish away with you. Even organic waste such as apple cores is best not left lying around as it can upset the diet of animals and birds and spoil things for other visitors.
- Please don't pick any fruit or flowers.
- Do make an effort to learn some Portuguese. Rest assured it will be appreciated. *Bom dia* is 'good morning', *por favor* 'please' and *olá* 'hello'. 'Thank you' when spoken by a man is *obrigado*, for a woman *obrigada*. English is widely spoken but don't take it for granted. It's polite to check 'Do you speak English?' *Você fala inglês?* Appendix C is a glossary of terms commonly found on maps and signs.
- Lastly, don't leave your common sense at home.

EMERGENCIES

For medical matters, walkers who live in the EU need a European Health Insurance Card (EHIC) while UK residents require a UK Global Health Insurance Card (GHIC). Holders of both are entitled to emergency and medical treatment in Portugal on a par with the locals. A small fee may be levied. English is widely spoken among medical personnel and at chemists. Non-EU nationals need to check if their country has a reciprocal agreement with Portugal and take out suitable cover if it doesn't. In any case travel insurance to cover a walking holiday is warmly recommended as rescue and repatriation costs can be hefty.

The following services may be of help should problems arise:

tel 112 for all emergencies

tel 117 to report forest fires

'Help!' in Portuguese is *socorro!* or *ajuda!* (pronounced 'i-you-da') while *perigo* ('pair-ee-go') is 'danger'.

USING THIS GUIDE

In this guide the Rota Vicentina is described in the north–south direction, however there is absolutely no reason why the route cannot be walked in the opposite direction. Waymarking is bi-directional and stage times are virtually the same.

Moreover, by no means do walkers have to follow the trek as described here metre by metre. The Rota Vicentina lends itself perfectly to individually tailored holidays. New variants are continually being added – see the Rota Vicentina website for new ideas. The route summary at the beginning of the book shows distances and timing at a glance and will come in helpful here. Remember that every stage ends with accommodation possibilities, plus transport. A taxi

is never far away; they can come in handy should you wish to skip a stage, deal with bad weather or even have luggage carried ahead.

Whatever way you go, a rest day – or two – can double as the opportunity to catch up on washing and diary entries, as well as look around and learn a little more about the area and village you're in, without forgetting taking well-earned time out at one of the superb Alentejo or Algarve beaches. The list of stopovers is temptingly long but suggestions include Porto Covo, Vila Nova de Milfontes and Carrapateira, as well as the surfing village of Sagres at the trek end.

In the route descriptions useful landmarks that appear on the map are shown in **bold**, the Rota Vicentina is abbreviated as RV, the Historical Way section as HW and the Fishermen's Trail section as FT. Compass directions are abbreviated as S (for south), N (for north) and so on.

Each walk stage is preceded by an information box containing the following essential data:

- **Start**
- **Distance** in kilometres
- **Ascent and Descent** This is important information, as height gain and loss are an indication of effort required and need to be taken into account alongside difficulty and distance when planning the day.
- **Difficulty** Each stage has been classified by grade, although

adverse weather conditions will make even a stroll more arduous. Grade 1 means an easy route on clear tracks and paths, suitable for beginners. Grade 2 is used for paths across hill and mountain terrain, with plenty of ups and downs; a reasonable level of fitness is preferable. The Rota Vicentina never exceeds Grade 2.

- **Walking time** This does not include pauses for picnics, admiring views and flowers, taking photos or nature stops, so as a general rule add on a couple of hours when planning your day. In warm weather you'll definitely want to factor in time for swimming at the inviting beaches and coves along the coast. Approximate timings for sections of each stage are shown in brackets, in hours and minutes.
- **Refreshments** Places along the way where a drink, snack and possibly a meal can be enjoyed.
- **Accommodation** Location of places to overnight en route.

GPX tracks

GPX tracks for the routes in this guidebook are available to download free at www.cicerone.co.uk/1143/GPX. A GPS device is an excellent aid to navigation, but you should also carry a map and compass and know how to use them. GPX files are provided in good faith, but neither the author nor the publisher accepts responsibility for their accuracy.

THE ROTA
VICENTINA

One of the marvellous accessible beaches on the outskirts of Zambujeira do Mar (Stage 6)

STAGE 1
Santiago do Cacém to Moinhos do Paneiro

Start	Santiago do Cacém bus station
Distance	21km
Ascent	280m
Descent	315m
Grade	1–2
Walking time	5hr 10min
Refreshments	Vale Seco
Accommodation	Vale Seco, Moinhos do Paneiro

The Rota Vicentina strikes out as the red/white-marked Historical Way leaving Santiago do Cacém to head due south on a series of clear lanes and paths. Walkers are led across rolling rural landscapes dotted with farms and through vast cork oak woods typical of the Alentejo region, with occasional promising glimpses of the coast and the sparkling Atlantic Ocean (three days off). After dropping in at a peaceful farming village, this opening stage concludes at fascinating old windmills with comfortable accommodation, although there is another overnight option 20min before the end.

Seeing as this is the opening stage you'll undoubtedly be very excited, however as it is the very first day on the trail with a rucksack, in all likelihood it will feel long and tiring. Do take your time.

SANTIAGO DO CACÉM

Santiago do Cacém, where the Rota Vicentina adventure begins, is a typical township in the rural Alentejo region. Its old centre features steep cobbled streets leading up to a fortified castle atop a prominent hill. The town became part of Portugal in 1217 and the king handed it over to the custodianship of the Santiago order of warrior monks, hence the first part of the name. Cacém on the other hand derives from Kassen, as the settlement was previously known under the Moors.

The town has plenty of facilities including restaurants and shops. Places to stay include centrally located Residencial Covas (tel 269 822675) and Hotel Dom Nuno (tel 269 823325 http://hoteldomnuno.com).

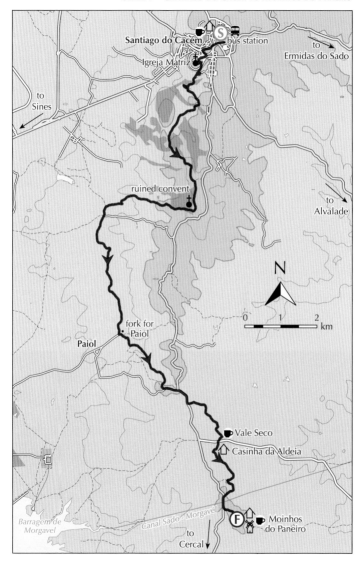

This is the official start of the Rota Vicentina and signposts and clear red/white markings appear here to guide you on your way.

From the bus station at **Santiago do Cacém** walk SW up to cross the main road then keep R up a street at the foot of a park. At the corner go L and up to where cobbled way Rua Dr Francesco Beja Costa branches R. Following signs for the Centro Histórico it's uphill to a T-junction then L past the tourist office. Not far along is the main church **Igreja Matriz (15min)** alongside the *castelo*, home to screeching swifts and zooming swallows. It occupies a marvellous position dominating the plains. ◄

Remember to look back to Santiago and its castle.

You're pointed down a flight of steps to traverse a park with a swimming pool and WC. Paths lead through woodland and up to join a series of lanes leading mostly S. Tiny smallholdings are passed, as are grazing sheep and the first of the many cork oaks. ◄

At a modest farm you change direction and take a path W past the ruins of a 15th-century **convent (1hr 30min)** before lanes resume through land planted with eucalypts. There are vast views towards the coast and over the port of Sines and its power station in the distance. The way drops into a lovely valley thick with rock roses, before gradually bearing S again mostly on a level in the company of cork oaks and the odd farm.

Cork trees on the way to Vale Seco

At a surfaced road and a **fork** (for Paiol) you veer sharp L and down into a shady flowered valley, heading

An old windmill at Moinhos do Paneiro, stage end

mostly SE. ▶ Up on a rise at a lane is a wide ridge with pylons and cultivated fields. A surfaced road is joined R for 5min before you're pointed off L through to a cluster of rural houses that go by the name of **Vale Seco (2hr 40min)**. A welcome café-cum-grocery shop completes the laidback picture.

By turning R you quickly reach the main road. Cross straight over onto a lane past houses and farms. Not far along where the route veers R are cypress trees and the entrance to Casinhas da Aldeia accommodation (https://casinhas-da-aldeia.negocio.site/, tel 926 135594/962 284363, fatima.krus@gmail.com, meals available if requested in advance). Continue on essentially S to join the road briefly. You soon leave it for a lane L and go over a rise to **Moinhos do Paneiro (45min)**.

Here are marvellous twin windmills dating back to the mid 1800s; the adjoining buildings provide accommodation (tel 269 909047/937 184176 **www.moinhosdopaneiro.com**, meals available if requested in advance).

En route are a number of stock gates that need to be closed after you.

37

STAGE 2
Moinhos do Paneiro to Cercal do Alentejo

Start	Moinhos do Paneiro
Distance	20km
Ascent	160m
Descent	215m
Grade	1
Walking time	4hr 30min
Refreshments	Vale das Éguas
Accommodation	Cercal do Alentejo

Still as the HW, the Rota Vicentina presses on with easy-going rambling mostly on lanes through well-kept farmland in rolling countryside with cork oak woods as far as the vast expanse of the Barragem de Campilhas reservoir. Perfect for picnics and even a cooling dip, it was constructed in 1954 for irrigation purposes and usually fills up during the rainy winter months. A little further on, the day's destination, Cercal do Alentejo, is a typical rural town with low-set whitewashed houses and good amenities.

This lovely stretch passes through open fields alive with wildflowers and songbirds alternating with stands of eucalypts and conifers.

From **Moinhos do Paneiro**, keep walking along the lane you arrived on, heading E along a lush valley with a marshy lake, before more rural landscapes and farms with pigs and cows. Wheat fields accompany the way up to the road into the sleepy settlement of **Vale das Éguas** (**1hr 20min**) with a café-restaurant that specialises in BBQ pork. After a second café on the roadside, lanes take over through rolling farmland and across a road. ◄

You touch on the northernmost end of the sprawling artificial lake before heading out to join a road. Turn R past the Monte do Arneiro property and on to pick up a dirt track on the R, parallel to the road. The inviting lakeside is not far away so by all means leave the track for a while and head through to the water's edge of the **Barragem de Campilhas**; a small inlet doubles as a splendid picnic spot. Water level permitting, stick with the lakeside all the way

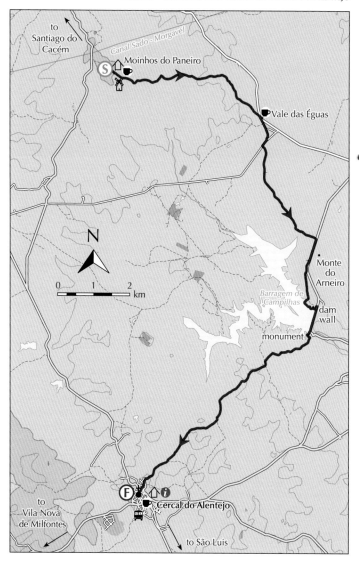

Lanes lead towards the Barragem de Campilhas

around to where you rejoin the track. It's not far on to the road over the **dam wall** (**1hr 30min**) which you cross to the far end with a **monument** to the reservoir's construction.

Now it's decidedly uphill for a leisurely stretch SW through farmland. Further on you saunter past outlying homes before entering the narrow streets lined by white houses of sleepy **Cercal do Alentejo** (**1hr 50min**). Walk through to the main road and cross straight over to reach the **church**, where the stage officially ends. Turn L here for accommodation at Azul Alentejano, only metres before the main square and roundabout.

Tourist office (tel 269 904187 turismo@cm-santi agocacem.pt), Rede Expressos buses to Lisbon, Rodoviária buses to Milfonte and Odemira, shops, restaurants; Stay at the hotel Azul Alentejano tel 269 949227 http://azulalentejanohotel.com/ or take a room at Baú Doce tel 269 904116 or 964 261055 above the excellent pastelaria (cake shop/café) in the main square.

Note: Cercal do Alentejo marks the spot where the RV splits: the main HW continues south for four stages inland to Odeceixe – this is described in the reverse direction in Stages 1IR–4IR in this guide. Another branch goes west to the coast and Porto Covo for the start of the Fishermen's Trail – as in the following stage.

STAGE 3
Cercal do Alentejo to Porto Covo

Start	Cercal do Alentejo church
Distance	16.5km
Ascent	185m
Descent	290m
Grade	1
Walking time	4hr 15min
Refreshments	Pouca Farinha
Accommodation	Herdade da Matinha, Cabeça da Cabra, Porto Covo

Today the RV enters the vast Parque Natural do Sudoeste Alentejano e Costa Vicentina and stays in it all the way down to Cabo de São Vicente. This varied stage initially heads west through farmland gradually dropping to the coastal plain and veering north before setting its sights on the Atlantic coast. It's very exciting to reach the ocean and the stage conclusion at the picturesque fishing village of Porto Covo.

From the **church** at **Cercal do Alentejo** follow the arrows through the maze of narrow streets looping S then steadily W. You leave the built-up area past old wash troughs and embark on country lanes into the surrounding countryside. Fields and well-kept farmhouses are the norm at first. A eucalypt plantation precedes upmarket country hotel **Herdade da Matinha** (tel 933 739245 www.herdadedamatinha.com). Lanes continue through bracken and aromatic shrubs to a rise where all of a sudden the Atlantic Ocean comes into view.

An especially pleasant drawn-out descent leads to well-kept crops where you are pointed R (N) past fields, over the **Corgo dos Godins river** and onto tarmac in view of one of the many wind farms set back from this coast. Further along signs send you veering L onto a shady lane to houses and an old school now upmarket

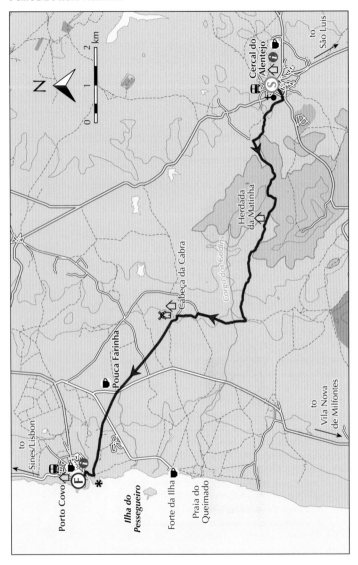

guesthouse Cabeça da Cabra (tel 966 295432 https://cabecadacabra.com). Then you pass an old windmill, its sail long gone.

Follow signs and waymarks carefully as you're pointed by fields, woods and streams and across a road to the laidback village of **Pouca Farinha** with its café (3hr 15min). Then it's over a minor road as you make a beeline WNW for the coast at last. The HW joins

A lovely stretch on the way to the coast

The tiny harbour at Porto Covo

forces with the green-blue waymarked FT not far from a **lookout**.

Now you look over to the whitewashed buildings and orange roofs of your inviting destination. Turn R to dip across a stream near a tiny harbour before a steepish street leads up to a small square with the tourist office of picturesque **Porto Covo** (1hr).

Tourist info (tel 269 959120 turismo.portocovo@ gmail.com), Rede Expressos buses to Lisbon and Zambujeira do Mar, shops, restaurants; stay at centrally located Zé Inàcio (tel 269 959136 zeinacio. portocovo@gmail.com) or Ahoy Hostel (tel 269 959014 **www.ahoyportocovohostel.com**).

STAGE 4

Porto Covo to Vila Nova de Milfontes

Start	Porto Covo tourist office
Distance	20km
Ascent	160m
Descent	160m
Grade	1
Walking time	5hr 15min
Refreshments	Forte da Ilha, Ponta das Barcas
Accommodation	Vila Nova de Milfontes

A simply spectacular day out on the coast in the company of the magnificent Atlantic Ocean, inviting beaches, dramatic cliffs, bright wildflowers and hardy sea birds. The historic Forte da Ilha do Pessegueiro (usually shortened to Forte da Ilha) and a welcoming café-resto await on the glorious beachfront where a swim is definitely called for – allow for extra time today.

Alternating with clifftop paths are inland tracks traversing the undeveloped plain parallel to the coast. It is rather tiring as you'll be walking on sandy terrain and shade is a rare luxury so go prepared with abundant sun protection and drinking water. While there are no technical difficulties, strong winds could make the cliff paths risky so take care and keep well back from the edge. The memorable day wraps up at Vila Nova de Milfontes, a lovely small town on the estuary of the Rio Mira river where Hannibal reputedly took shelter.

The stage begins at the Porto Covo tourist information office

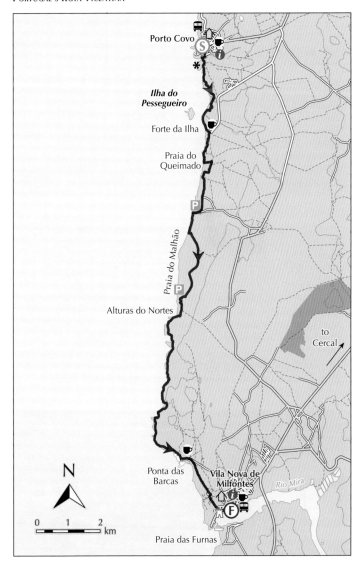

Porto Covo

*

*Ilha do
Pessegueiro*

Forte da Ilha

Praia do
Queimado

Praia do Malhão

Alturas do Nortes

to
Cercal

N

0   1   2
km

Ponta das
Barcas

Vila Nova de
Milfontes

Rio Mira

Praia das Furnas

From the tourist office at **Porto Covo** take the steepish street SE down across the stream (the way you arrived in Stage 3) and up the other side to where the HW and FT part ways. Keep R on the FT branch with green-blue markers past an excellent lookout and onto a boardwalk. This proceeds along the low clifftops touching on secluded coves, to where the glorious Praia da Ilha beach is joined near the island Ilha do Pessegueiro. Continue along the sand to **Forte da Ilha** (1hr) and its inviting café-resto.

> The adjacent **fort** dates back to 1588. Designed by an Italian architect, it was intended to prevent attacks from English pirates. Immediately offshore is

Praia da Ilha backed by the Ilha do Pessegueiro

the fortified island of Ilha do Pessegueiro. Occupied by the Carthaginians in the third century BC, the Romans later used it as a fishing port complete with tanks for salting fish.

The well-marked FT leads along the lane behind the old fort before veering R as a beautiful path along clifftops through masses of flowering plants to the sandy expanse of **Praia do Queimado**. Not far from a house you're pointed briefly inland to cross a stream then you need to follow low pole markers carefully to join a sandy lane over consolidated dunes parallel to the beach. ◄

At low tide when the sea is calm, by all means walk along the beach all the way to Praia do Malhão where wooden stairs lead back up to the marked trail.

Around 2km further on is a building and **car park** used by surfers, as well as a stream. Here the lovely cliff path resumes, followed by a 3km sandy piste where the occasional pine tree spells sparse shade. At a large **car park (1hr 40min)** at **Praia do Malhão** the path returns once more to the glorious seafront with boardwalks and

Looking back onto glorious Praia do Malhão

benches, perfect for picnics. (For those who can't resist the call of the sea, flights of wooden stairs lead down to the golden sand.)

The path leads inevitably due S high over the coast to where the end of the beach marks the beginning of the rugged **Alturas do Nortes** sandstone cliffs and the first of the sea stacks which double as nesting places for acrobatic storks. ▶ A spectacular section runs high over a string of inaccessible sand-pebble coves before bearing gradually SE to **Ponta das Barcas** aka Canal (**1hr 45min**) with a café-restaurant.

The route proceeds along a quiet road above a modest fishing harbour, and is soon pointed onto a lane. At a cluster of new houses bear R through empty lots and past houses and hotels. You emerge on Avenida Marginal and the wonderful waterfront of **Vila Nova de Milfontes** (**50min**) with another beckoning beach.

Marvellous spreads of wildflowers shelter near the seafront

Here the rocky-sandy ground is lined with rabbit tracks and carpeted with Hottentot fig plants sporting bright pink blooms.

49

At **Vila Nova de Milfontes** the picturesque mouth of the Rio Mira river spreads out; once navigable for 30km inland to Odemira. There's also a modest castle, Forte de São Clemente, draped with palms; it was built in the late 1500s to protect the village from pirate attacks. The town's claim to fame nowadays is as the largest resort on the Alentejo coast, although in comparison to the crowds of the Algarve region, it's decidedly laidback, especially in walking season. The name derives from 'a thousand fountains' due to its myriad watercourses and underground springs.

Tourist info (tel 283 996599 **https://turismo.cm-odemira.pt**), shops, restaurants, Rede Expressos bus services to both Lisbon and Lagos. Sleep at Casa da Adro (tel 917 171811 **www.casadoadro.com.pt**) or Blue Guide rooms (tel 968 780680 blueguidegh@gmail.com, stayinalentejo@gmail.com).

STAGE 5

Vila Nova de Milfontes to
Almograve

Start	Vila Nova de Milfontes castle
Distance	15km
Ascent	130m
Descent	150m
Grade	1–2
Walking time	4hr 30min (3hr 15min if you take the river ferry)
Refreshments	Furnas
Accommodation	Almograve

The opening section of this stage is not terribly interesting as it follows busy roads before crossing the broad Rio Mira on a sleek bridge constructed in 1974. However this is easily avoidable thanks to a handy family-run boat taxi from the jetty below the castle at Vila Nova de Milfontes (tel 964 200944, operates daily 9am–6pm except Dec and Jan). The toy-like traditional fishing boat potters across the river to Furnas, a fun way to begin the stage and one that cuts 1hr 15min off the day's load.

Thereafter comes a relaxing inland stretch in the company of shady shrubs and farmland before a return to the coast to be rewarded with pristine Brejo Largo beach, a real treat! At day's end is Almograve, a sleepy town with decent amenities.

From the castle (Forte de São Clemente) on the river at **Vila Nova de Milfontes** take the road Rua Barbosa Viana up to the whitewashed church then keep up Rua Sarmento Beires, proceeding past shops and a cinema to the *escola primaria* and tourist office. Continue walking in the same direction (NE) along the main road Rua Custódio Brás Pacheco for 1.5km all the way to the major **roundabout** where it's R and across the landmark road bridge over the Rio Mira.

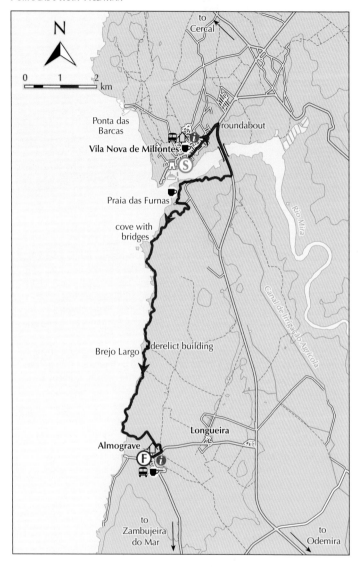

The ferry crossing Rio Mira

Over the other side don't miss the FT fork R. A path leads through peaceful fields and woodland with abandoned buildings, and heads down to Furnas (**1hr 15min**) on the riverside with a first café near a landing stage. A lane L leads parallel to the beach, **Praia das Furnas**. ▶ At a second café (Ocean Drive Beach Club) the FT turns L (E) up a minor road and not far up forks R (SW) on a lane between fields and acacia trees, soon parallel to the coast. Further along a signed path R heads back to the sea, over low clay cliffs. You drop across a pebbly cove on timber bridges.

Due to the jagged rocky coastline now the path stays slightly inland on consolidated sand dunes. After a long stretch of lane flanking turf fields a sharp R sees you walking through a veritable tunnel of low acacia trees with purple carpets of Hottentot fig. Back close to the ocean are thickets of reeds around a couple of footbridges and soon a **derelict building**. A third footbridge marks the point where you cross to sand dunes and the edge of the magnificent long **Brejo Largo** beach (**1hr 45min**).

It's well worth popping over the boardwalk through to the glorious stretch of sand.

Crossing sand dunes en route to Brejo Largo

Here the official FT route leads easily along the clifftop. (For walkers who can't resist the pull of a simply gorgeous beach, steep steps plunge down crumbly dark inclines to the water's edge. Watch your step! About half-way along the beachfront a rope-aided rail leads back up to rejoin the official path.) The delightful ensuing stretch passes high above several more beaches as well as rugged reefs, before finally veering inland. A lane around fields and across a stream is followed by a R turn on the road past the youth hostel and tourist office and into **Almograve (1hr 30min)**.

Tourist info (tel 283 647643 **https://turismo.cm-odemira.pt**), shops, restaurants, Rede Expressos bus to Lisbon. Accommodation at the hostel Pousada da Juventude (tel 283 010532 **https://pousadasjuventude.pt**) or Almograve Beach Hostel (tel 963 373635).

STAGE 6
Almograve to
Zambujeira do Mar

Start	Almograve
Distance	22km
Ascent	110m
Descent	100m
Grade	1–2
Walking time	6hr
Refreshments	Praia do Almograve, Cavaleiro, Entrada da Barca
Accommodation	Zambujeira do Mar

Another great day on the trail. The opening section as far as Cabo Sardão, approximately halfway, is especially wonderful thanks to the surprising number of stork nests on precipitous cliff edges and sea stacks, undeniably one of the top highlights of the Rota Vicentina. Afterwards comes a long rather monotonous track to a tiny picturesque fishing harbour. All fatigue is forgotten thanks to the superb conclusion at the beautiful bay of beachfront Zambujeira do Mar.

Note: at the walk start you'll be forgiven for shortcutting to the coast by taking the road directly out to Praia do Almograve, saving around 15min.

From the roundabout at **Almograve** go R as signed for Centro. At the church keep R again following waymarks and soon L above the river. A path leads past the water treatment plant and out to the rocky seafront. There you bear L towards lovely Praia do Almograve and along a boardwalk to a **car park**. A turn R sees you on a dirt road heading S overlooking the Atlantic and the beautiful beach. ▶

Along the way are keep fit points.

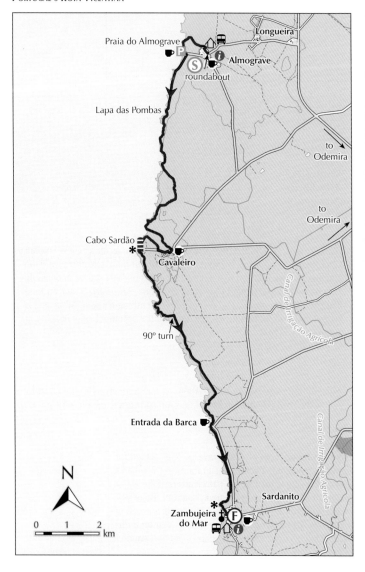

You pass a slender promontory with photogenic fishing cabins and continue to where the road starts to drop (to the tiny fishing harbour **Lapa das Pombas**) – here the FT strikes out on a path across bright red sand colonised by hardy Mediterranean plants. You're never far back from the dark rugged coastline of massive slabs. A brief detour inland traverses consolidated sand dunes with pines and eucalypts. Keep your eyes peeled for waymarks at the many forks. The return to the coast means dramatic yellow and white cliffs, quite spectacular. Not far along the FT swerves decidedly SE on a dirt track to the laid-back village of **Cavaleiro (2hr 45min)** where there are cafés and shops.

A road leads due W at first before a path R takes over to round the point to the 1915 lighthouse on **Cabo Sardão**, where awesomely inclined sheer schist cliffs are home to a huge colony of nonchalant storks. ▸ Then head along the wide sandy cycle track S through low trees and masses of scented white rock rose shrubs and past a string of lookouts.

Dramatic white and yellow cliffs precede Cavaleiro

Don't miss the Miradouro Sardão with helpful info boards about local flora and fauna.

57

Magnificent cliff scenery near Cabo Sardão

Further along at an info board about bird life the FT takes a **90° turn** R, embarking on a dead straight stretch in a rural ambience. Ahead in the distance are greenhouses, a sea of white. Further on a fork R leads back closer to the coast, and not far on a steep path and steps plunge to a small fishing harbour. A minor road leads up to old-style fishing cabins, a radar station and a cluster of inviting café-restaurants at **Entrada da Barca** (**2hr 30min**).

Now the path runs alongside the road SSE for 2km. Just as it reaches the edge of Zambujeira do Mar, fork R for a wonderful conclusion on a boardwalk leading over more spectacular cliffs and dunes. Enjoy views both up and down the coast to beaches, including one accessible by a steep stairway. After a **lookout** platform the FT walks straight into laidback **Zambujeira do Mar** (**45min**) and its tiny plaza and Nossa Senhora do Mar chapel dominating another gorgeous bay. ◄

The marvellous place name means 'wild olive tree on the sea'.

Tourist info (tel 283 961144 **https://turismo.cm-odemira.pt**), shops, restaurants, Rede Expressos buses to Vila Nova de Milfontes and Lisbon. Overnight options include Hostel Hakuna Matata (tel 918 470038) and Ondazul (tel 283 961450 **http://ondazul.zambujeira-do-mar.hotels-pt.net/it/**).

STAGE 7
Zambujeira do Mar to Odeceixe

Start	Zambujeira do Mar seafront chapel
Distance	18km
Ascent	280m
Descent	310m
Grade	2
Walking time	5hr
Refreshments	Praia do Carvalhal, Azenha do Mar
Accommodation	Odeceixe

An excellent varied stage that spends just about all day close to the ocean with dramatic cliffs and visits to inviting beaches, without forgetting quite a fair few ups and downs and some narrow steep hands-on stretches. Spectacular scenery is the flavour of the day.

Halfway along is the fishing hamlet Azenha do Mar with a local seafood restaurant, a great favourite with the Portuguese for its rice casseroles and goose barnacles; bottom line: plan on arriving well before midday if you want a table for lunch.

On the other hand Odeceixe, the day's destination, is a cosy friendly river town with plenty of accommodation. Located a tad inland, it marks the point where the main RV trek leaves the Alentejo region to enter the Algarve. It also marks the conclusion of the FT. Moreover, for walkers who opt for a circuit route, this is the place where the inland route begins – looping back up to Cercal do Alentejo on the northbound HW – see Stages 1IR–4IR.

Note: this stage concludes with 4km along a road, albeit quiet and following a river. Should you prefer to avoid it, ask your accommodation provider in Odeceixe to arrange for a taxi.

From the seafront chapel at **Zambujeira do Mar** head down to the beautiful main beach then take the path

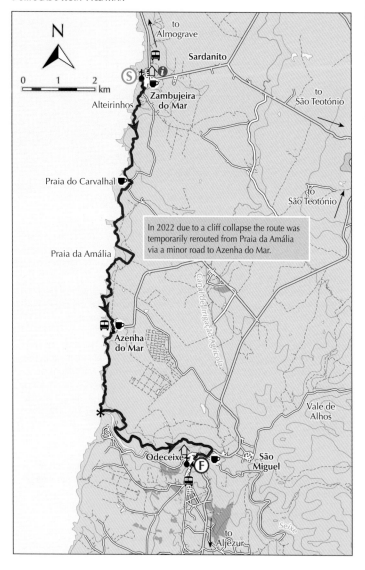

N

0   1   2 km

to
Almograve

Sardanito

S

Zambujeira
do Mar

Alteirinhos

to
São Teotónio

Praia do Carvalhal

to
São Teotónio

In 2022 due to a cliff collapse the route was
temporarily rerouted from Praia da Amália
via a minor road to Azenha do Mar.

Praia da Amália

Canal de Irrigação Agrícola

Azenha
do Mar

Vale de
Alhos

Odeceixe

São
Miguel

F

Seixe

to
Aljezur

cutting uphill past a line of low-lying houses on the headland. Soon a long wooden staircase descends to **Alteirinhos**, an official nudist beach, although the FT leaves the steps before the bottom, forking L across a stream and cutting across a cliff flank on a marvellously scenic stretch. A brief detour inland crosses sandy terrain through woodland dominated by conifers and acacias, quickly returning coastwards via a boardwalk. Close by is a headland over an inlet. The path plunges to a car park and surf school-cum-café at **Praia do Carvalhal (1hr)**.

Head uphill alongside fences belonging to a wildlife park, and on to a dramatic white headland. Soon a narrow path plunges to a saddle on a promontory then climbs through bracken past the top of a small waterfall via a batch of minor bridges. An abrupt detour inland features fields and greenhouses before a tunnel of bushes over a stream and the seafront with the stunning beach **Praia da Amália**. ▸

You cross a stream and resume the clifftop high above rugged coves the rest of the way to the tiny village **Azenha do Mar (1hr 50min)** with its memorable restaurant (tel 282 947297) and bus stop. Both fishing and seaweed harvesting are practised at this village.

Leaving Alteirinhos behind, the path cuts around the cliff

The beach was named afrer Portugal's most famous fado singer, Amália Rodrigues, who reportedly learned to swim here.

The path descends towards the harbour with a slippery final stretch before climbing quite steeply to a headland to resume the lovely cliff walk due S accompanied by masses of glorious wildflowers. En route are attractive bays and surf beaches, then all of a sudden you find yourself on a promontory **lookout** (**1hr**) above the stunningly photogenic estuary and sandbanks of the Seixe river, opposite a beach and houses.

The FT veers L (SE) inland through fields and down a rough lane to the tranquil verdant riverside. The final 4km, in the company of rushes, giant fennel plants and marsh orchids, are surfaced. Once out at the main road turn R for the bridge over the Seixe. ◄ On the other side go R again off the main road then next L into **Odeceixe** (**1hr 10min**) and its charming square.

As you do so you're leaving the Alentejo region to enter the Algarve.

Odexeice appears along the Seixe river

Shops, restaurants, Rede Expressos bus to Lisbon, EVA Transportes bus to Aljezur and Lagos, Rodoviário to Santiago do Cacém. Accommodation includes Hospedaria Firmino Bernardino (tel 282 947362) and Odeceixe Hostel (tel 913 919357).

STAGE 8
Odeceixe to Aljezur

Start	Odeceixe main square
Distance	19km
Ascent	100m
Descent	100m
Grade	1–2
Walking time	5hr 15min
Refreshments	Rogil
Accommodation	Rogil, Aljezur

Marked red/white as per the HW, the RV proceeds inexorably on its way south. Taking a temporary break from the dramatic coast it traverses flatter countryside inland, touching on irrigation channels and the well-served village of Rogil. At day's end in a fertile river valley is the attractive fortified village of Aljezur boasting the ruins of a 10th-century Moorish castle offering great views and fascinating history – it is one of the seven castles depicted on the Portuguese flag. If you're too tired after today's exertions, make the most of the short stage tomorrow to take time out for the castle visit.

▶ From **Odeceixe** and the main square (Largo 1° de Maio) follow the red/white waymarks S but at the first corner don't miss the turn sharp R onto the narrow alley Rua do Outão up to Rua 25 Abril. At the church branch L up steps and cobbled streets, puffing all the way to a lookout with an old **windmill**. Then it's past a string of traditional low-set houses.

You keep straight on through laid-back Malhadais with its water tanks to an abrupt turn L past playing fields and out to the main road, following red/white waymarks carefully (nb don't be tempted by the red/yellow markings of a circular route). A long stretch S traverses agricultural land with farms and stands of eucalypts and pines trees. Bearing mostly SW the way returns to the road and

An FT variant from Odeceixe leads via the coast before looping back to Rogil. It adds on 3km and involves a little road walking.

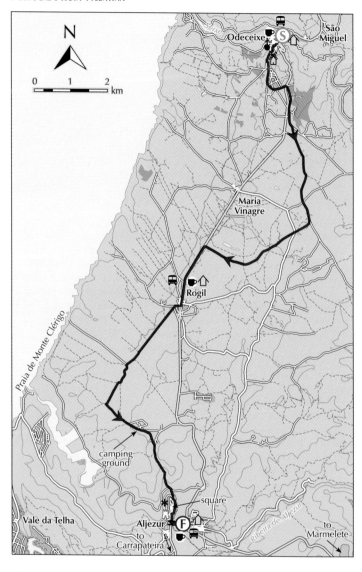

Odeceixe's square

runs alongside it to a lovely café-restaurant ▶ on the outskirts of **Rogil** (2hr 15min).

The HW follows the main road through Rogil (served by EVA Transportes buses) lined with shops and houses. (Accommodation at Alcatruz Hotel tel 282 998203 www.hotelalcatruz.com). After a fountain decorated with gigantic goose barnacles you're pointed R then sharp L. Accompanied by low shrubby vegetation and woodland a sequence of minor roads and lanes proceed SW, within earshot of the sea.

You veer SE past a large **camping ground** before descending through trees to the valley of the Ribeira de Aljezur. Cross the bridge over the river. At a nearby signed intersection at the foot of a hill keep L – as per red/yellow signs for Porto de Aljezur. A gentle uphill stretch soon sees you in the old elongated village hilltop settlement of **Aljezur**, where the square hosts a prominent statue of Henry the Navigator and helpful bilingual boards explain the original function of the village's elegant low-set whitewashed buildings. (A detour R leads up to the castle belvedere.) Continue straight ahead down the cobbled streets to a café and footbridge (**3hr**). ▶

This offers local specialities such as caracóis (snails) and cakes made with batata doce(sweet potato), a nice change from that usual lunchtime sandwich.

An elegant medieval bridge spanned the river here until it was washed away by floodwaters in 1947.

The name **Aljezur** probably derives from the Arabic for 'island' in view of its elongated peninsula shape surrounded by watercourses; the town was under Moorish rule until 1249, and was the very last in Algarve to be conquered by the Christians. According to local hearsay the knights who finally overran the castle were fuelled by a stew concocted with local beans and *batata doce* (although the sweet potato wasn't actually discovered – in America – until two centuries later!) Its ancient port, protected by the castle, spelled direct access to the sea. Now silted up, the river that once flowed here was an essential transport artery for Aljezur to trade its agricultural products with ports as far apart as Flanders and the African coast. The river also powered mills to grind the region's cereals.

Shops, restaurants, Rede Expressos bus to Sagres and Lisbon, EVA Transportes bus to Carrapateira, Lagos and Odeceixe. Overnight options: Amazigh Hostel (tel 282 997502 www.amazighostel. com) or rooms at Guesthouse A Lareira (tel 282 998440), a 10min walk from the old town.

Prince Henry the Navigator greets walkers in Aljezur

STAGE 9
Aljezur to Arrifana

Start	Footbridge at Aljezur
Distance	12km
Ascent	170m
Descent	160m
Grade	1
Walking time	3hr
Refreshments	None until the end
Accommodation	Arrifana

This relatively short stage makes its roller-coaster way across lovely open hilly landscapes with flourishing flowering shrub vegetation and watercourses. The day ends at marvellous seaside Arrifana – not a village as such but a fishing harbour overlooked by a historic fort and a handful of cafés and places to stay near a wonderful beach that is popular with surfers and easily visitable in view of the brevity of the stage. Otherwise a marvellous optional circuit loops via panoramic Ponta da Atalaia (Watchtower Point), once an ancient Roman site; it lengthens the day's load by 2hr and 7km – see below.

A final option exclusively for ultra-fit walkers entails skipping Arrifana (a great pity) by turning S from the last junction and ploughing on for Carrapateira – a grand total of 8hr.

From the **footbridge** at the base of **Aljezur** walk up the cobbled street to the square with the statue of Henry the Navigator, then branch L. Passing more low whitewashed buildings you climb surprisingly steeply to the main church. (Here a L turn will take you to the fascinating castle and lookout.) It's R at the church and soon heading W on a lane down into the valley of the Ribeira de Aljezur, the marshy expanse of the silted-up river thick with reeds interspersed with yellow flag flowers. An uphill stretch past houses leads through shrubs of cistus and tree heather. ▶

There are sweeping views to the sand dunes and coast with Amoreira and you get a good idea of the formerly navigable river once animated by sailing ships bound for Aljezur.

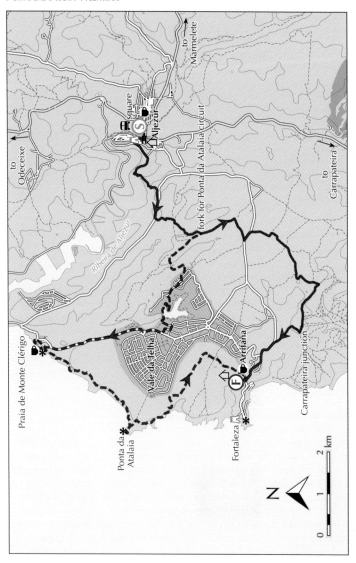

After a road crossing comes an undulating wide forestry track leading up to a farm and **fork** (**1hr**) where the optional Ponta da Atalaia circuit turns R.

Ponta da Atalaia circuit

With green/blue FT markings, tracks lead WNW touching on a lake before joining a road for 3km through sprawling **Vale da Telha**, a low-key housing estate. As it nears the coast you're pointed off L on a lane to a marvellous ocean **lookout**. (By all means detour R down to lovely **Praia de Monte Clérigo** for the beach and cafés.) On a lane then marvellous cliffside paths it's on to spectacular windswept **Ponta da Atalaia**. Further along a sheltered inland path plunges through shrub cover that includes dwarf palms and juniper, finally popping out at **Arrifana**, a tad uphill from the stage finish.

Arrifana beach

Lovely Praia de Monte Clérigo on the Ponta da Atalaia variant

The main route ignores the turn-off and heads S to another road where you branch decidedly L for a short stretch of tarmac. Past farms both active and abandoned and thickets of eucalypt trees, not to mention a glimpse of the promising sea, the HW traverses vast open rolling moorland with scrub shrubs and cushions of hardy flowers. A wonderfully desolate area.

At the signed **junction** (**1hr 30min**) – unless you opt to miss Arrifana and continue on to Carrapateira (a further 5hr 30min) – go R (NW) to where you join a road climbing through the outskirts past the modern hostel and continuing down to the car park where the stage ends overlooking the beach of **Arrifana** (**30min**).

Don't miss the signed detour to a magnificent lookout and the 1635 **Fortaleza**. Now a mere skeleton remains of the military structure ostensibly erected to protect the fish traps that would be set at the foot of the cliffs in summer when tuna were passing by. A tidal wave generated by the great 1755 earthquake all but devastated the site. Nearby is the fishermen's cooperative with its doll's-size cabins.

Cafés, restaurants, sleep at Hi Arrifana Hostel (tel 282 997455 **www.destinationhostels.com**), next door at Arrifana Lounge Guesthouse (tel 282 997496 **www.arrifanalounge.com**) or Boutique Guesthouse Releash Aljezur tel 963 984221 **https://releash-aljezur.com**.

STAGE 10

Arrifana to Carrapateira

Start	Arrifana
Distance	24km
Ascent	390m
Descent	480m
Grade	2
Walking time	6hr
Refreshments	Monte Novo, Bordeira
Accommodation	Monte Novo, Carrapateira

Today's stage is lengthy and rather tiring. It begins by dropping to a beautiful wild beach before rambling across undulating farmland and through woodland on a long-winded return to a superb stretch of coast with standout beaches and an inviting settlement. A handful of refreshment and accommodation options are encountered along the way should you wish to shorten the day.

The overall difficulty is given as Grade 2 in view of the duration in combination with multiple ups and downs as well as one possibly tricky stream crossing (only in the wake of heavy rain) just over 1hr into the walk, near Praia do Canal.

From **Arrifana** walk back along the road you came in along, SE and downhill to where the HW forks R on a clear trail. Past the **junction** with the route from Aljezur (Stage 9) it's not far down a steepish hillside to sea level. Here a **stream** needs crossing – in normal conditions you tiptoe across planks and stones, however after heavy rain you may need to take off your boots and wade across.

The reward for your efforts is the stunning beach of **Praia do Canal (1hr 15min)**, a vast expanse of sand backed by pebbles and Hottentot figs, miles away from anywhere. A couple of huts are the only signs of 'civilisation'. ▶

Offshore a curious pointed sea stack stands out.

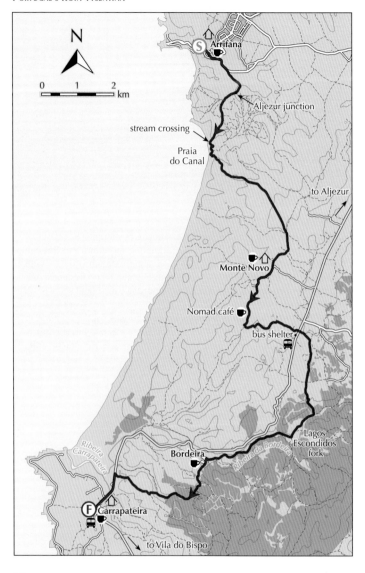

The HW doesn't tarry here but embarks on a broad track climbing SE away from the coast into a landscape dominated by eucalypts. A short section of sealed road in the vicinity of **Monte Novo** passes the premises of Barranco da Fonte (refreshments and B&B, tel 282 973223 www.barrancodafonte.pt, dinner available on request) then farmland with grazing livestock and barns. ▶

The way heads down towards Praia do Canal

Clear lanes continue past **Nomad cafè**, and downhill to dip into a sea of cistus shrubs then up and out to a road near a **bus shelter** (1hr 45min). You're halfway now!

Cross straight over for a quiet road S past vineyards, houses and fields down through woodland into the valley dotted with olive trees on farmland and run through by the Ribeira da Bordeira. The way bears R (W) past a farm building and **path fork** (for Lagos Escondidos – ignore this) before fording the river, usually a shallow affair. Further along, at the end of the valley, is the tiny village of **Bordeira** (**1hr 40min**) with an inviting café-restaurant and a pretty square boasting shady trees, welcome benches and a drinking fountain.

A FT variant soon breaks off R (SW) heading for the coast. Be aware that it entails a river crossing towards the end.

Now you go L, leaving the settlement and heading S up a hill back into scrubland, to the pounding of

Approaching Bordeira at last

not-so-distant waves. A never-ending roller-coaster track finally bears its reward when you reach a marvellous ridge looking over to the ocean and beckoning sandy beaches. A final descent concludes at a road where you go L across the river (Ribeira Carrapateira) and estuary to the spread-out village of **Carrapateira (1hr 20min)**.

This is a lovely spot for a **rest day** as there are several beaches to visit as well as a marked coastal walking track via the dramatic cliffs of Pontal da Carrapateira and Amado beach.

Shops, restaurants, Rede Expressos bus to Lisbon, EVA Transportes to Aljezur, accommodation at cosy Pensao das Dunas (tel 282 973118 **www.pensao-das-dunas.pt**) or centrally located Hostel do Mar (tel 960 269668 **https://hosteldomar.com**).

STAGE 11
Carrapateira to Vila do Bispo

Start	Carrapateira square
Distance	22km
Ascent	290m
Descent	220m
Grade	2
Walking time	5hr 10min
Refreshments	Pedralva
Accommodation	Pedralva, Vila do Bispo

This interesting day is spent inland on rugged terrain. The trek initially strikes out southeast making its way along the verdant valley of the Ribeira Carrapateira which it criss-crosses repeatedly. Important note: in normal conditions stepping stones keep your boots dry, however after heavy rain the river can swell and the flow with strong currents can prove dangerous. It may be necessary to follow the wet-weather variant given below from the Vilarinha junction – only marginally longer than the main route, it entails an extra 100m of ascent/descent.

If so desired the stage can be conveniently split into two by stopping over at charming Pedralva, just under halfway. A host of houses in this old Algarve village have been tastefully transformed into guest accommodation. A café and restaurant are part and parcel of the place.

From the **Carrapateira** square follow signs L at first to the upper village. Then continue past the local museum for a trail E along a wide panoramic ridge with an obelisk. The way descends into a valley to a house where an overgrown path R leads through to a wide lane in the delightful rural Ribeira Carrapateira valley. Further along S is the **Vilarinha junction** (**1hr 10min**) where the wet-weather variant breaks off R (see below).

In good weather stay with the main route, keeping L (E) past fields and through tree cover on a minor dirt road.

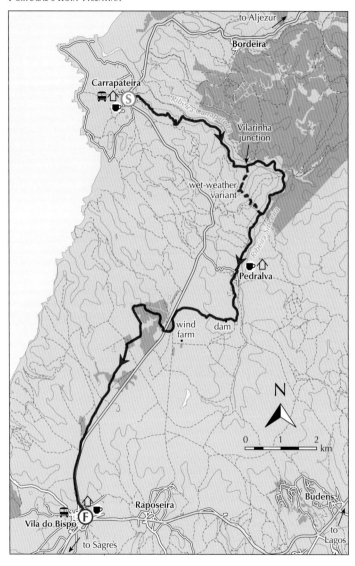

A stroll away from the junction is the first spot where the river is forded. Depending on conditions this will entail a simple crossing on stones or a paddle. It may be a good idea to take off your boots. You ford the river four times in rapid succession before branching R (S at first) into the minor valley of the **Ribeira Sinceira**. After a conifer copse this river also needs fording twice before the variant rejoins the main route.

Wet-weather variant
Leaving the main route at the **Vilarinha junction**, fork R along the lane to a cluster of holiday rental houses (this is Vilarinha proper). Walk straight on and go through a gate to where a narrow path continues before veering abruptly L. Now comes a steep overgrown uphill section in woodland. At the top veer L, this time in plunging descent. Watch your step on fallen branches and in no time you'll be down in the **Ribeira Sinceira** valley to pick up the main trail once again, turning R (SSW).

It's a straightforward stroll past scattered farms and houses to quiet **Pedralva** (**1hr 30min**). You're pointed up cobbled streets past a park with picnic tables and out the other side of the converted village to the inviting café-restaurant. (Accommodation – Aldeia da Pedralva, tel 282 639342 www.aldeiadapedralva.com.) You're almost halfway now.

Clearly marked lanes lead away from Pedralva back into farmed countryside, veering W past a small **dam**. ◄ You cross a main road to take a path dipping NW through strawberry trees into a shallow cool valley. A stiff climb leads to low scrubland peppered with clutches of shady conifers and the occasional eucalypt, on a never-ending traverse essentially S, soon parallel to the road. At last a water tower comes into sight, dominating the village that is today's destination nestling in a hollow sheltered from winds. Once you've reached the roadside walk down past the football stadium. At the bottom turn up L and keep your eyes peeled for the red/white waymarks that guide you through narrow paved streets to the central square of **Vila do Bispo** (**2hr 50min**), named for a 'bishop'.

Here the horizon is dominated by the giant propellers of a wind farm which dwarf mere walkers.

Stepping stones cross the Ribeira Carrapateira

Shops, cafés and restaurants, EVA Transportes bus to Sagres and Lagos, accommodation at Hotel Mira Sagres (tel 925 408080 **www.hotelmirasagres. com**) or Flor de Esteva (tel 916 868689 **https:// en.pureaccommodations.com/**).

The last leg to Vila do Bispo

STAGE 12
Vila do Bispo to Cabo de São Vicente

Start	Vila do Bispo square
Distance	14km
Ascent	80m
Descent	90m
Grade	1–2
Walking time	3hr 30min + 1hr 30min to Sagres
Refreshments	None until the end
Accommodation	Sagres

Cabo de São Vicente (Cape Saint Vincent) is an awe-inspiring spot to finish the marvellous Rota Vicentina trek. To get there the straightforward concluding stage of the HW takes an inland route, though it follows a lot of asphalt. However all is not lost as thankfully a FT variant provides a more exciting experience with a ramble along the dramatic coastline and dizzy clifftops. It is the same distance. Warning: in very high winds the variant could be dangerous and it is best to stick with the main route. Moreover, be aware that waymarking on the later section of the variant is not quite as frequent as usual.

Note: as there is nowhere to stay overnight at the stage conclusion, walkers need to proceed to Sagres, 6km away. Either take the bus, taxi or the FT route, a mix of clifftop and road walking (see below).

All around is an open heath plateau flooded by a sea of cistus plants, all but flattened by the prevailing winds that blast in from the Atlantic.

Leave the main square in **Vila do Bispo** following red/white paint marks downhill N to a bus stop. At the nearby roundabout turn L uphill near the *mercado* (market) and out of town along a quiet country road W. After 2km near a forestry station (**Casa do Guarda**) a dirt road takes over with views of Sagres in the distance S. Further on, past a weather station ignore the fork R (for **Torre do Aspa**, where a curious obelisk marks the highest elevation of the Costa Vicentina – a record 154m!). ◀

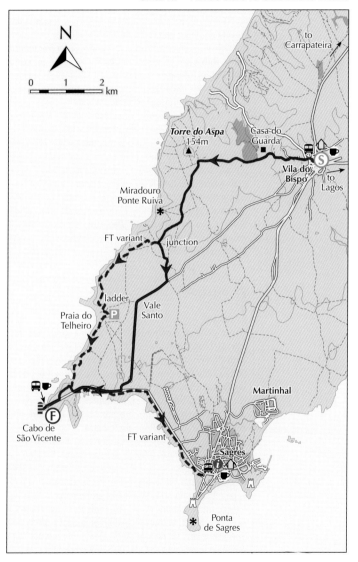

Branch L (SSW) with an exciting view towards the far-off lighthouse and Cabo de São Vicente, the day's destination and trek conclusion. Pass a detour for **Miradouro Ponte Ruiva** and continue on to the strategic **junction** (**1hr 30min**) for the recommended FT variant – see below.

The main route keeps L (S), soon a sandy path alongside a field and through to a lane where it's L again and soon R out to a wide dirt road. Now it's R (SW) across marshy terrain with reeds, dwarf palms and grazing cattle to the farm buildings of **Vale Santo**, the name a reference to an old pilgrimage route. Here you join a surfaced road S that leads out to the main Sagres–Cabo de São Vicente road where you turn R (W). With a short stretch of lane where the variant slips in, the final leg looks over to the breathtaking sheer towering cliffs and finally gains windblown **Cabo de São Vicente** (**2hr**) with its fortress, chapel, museum and huge landmark red lighthouse which is one of the most powerful in Europe, essential for shipping.

Facilities: snack bars, EVA Transportes bus to Sagres and Lagos.

FT variant

At the strategic **junction** turn R (W) on a sandy lane following blue/green waymarks through land smothered with domed mounds of yellow gorse. Where the lane ends a path takes over high above the sea in a dramatic landscape of eroding red-yellow cliffs and headlands. After a rocky section a short **ladder** helps you down a problem-free 1m drop. Not far on is a **car park** and access to the inviting **Praia do Telheiro**.

The signed path then visits a sheltered dip in the coastline which is home to a batch of dwarf palms. Back on the clifftop the vegetation is dominated by decidedly prostrate flowering plants, including rosemary. The underlying rock is pale limestone now. Waymarks are infrequent here but cairns, modest heaps of stones, show the way. There's a final beach well below (accessible on a goat path) before you join a lane to the road and turn R – in common with the main route – out to **Cabo de São Vicente** (**2hr**).

The ladder on the FT variant

Cabo de São Vicente, where it all comes to an end, is a magical spot. There are spectacular views over the dramatic Atlantic coast and wave-bashed cliffs. Nowadays it is famous as the southwestern extremity of mainland Europe and a hotspot for observing bird migrations in autumn. Together with the nearby promontory of Ponta de Sagres, it also happened to be the last bit of dry land Portuguese sailors and explorers would have seen as they headed off into the 'great unknown'. The windblown headlands and the end of the known world was a sacred place in the distant past for the Phoenicians, Greeks and Romans who called it Promontorium Sacrum; they reportedly believed that the sun hissed as it sank into the ocean off the cape. A mosque stood here during the later Moorish period. The cape took its present name from martyred Spanish deacon St Vincent, whose body washed up here; his tomb was guarded by ravens and became an important site of medieval pilgrimage. (He has since been shifted to Lisbon.)

FT route to Sagres

Follow the road away from the cape to where FT markers break off R near an old fort. This soon ducks back to the road before veering SE via dizzy clifftop paths. After you've cut across the neck of the long Pont de Sagres headland, a short stroll E is all that separates you from **Sagres** (1hr 30min).

Tourist office (tel 282 624873 **www.visitalgarve. pt**), shops, restaurants, cafés and accommodation for all pockets such as Lighthouse Hostel (tel 282 625341 **www.thelighthousehostel.com**) and Mareta Beach Boutique B&B (tel 282 620040 **www.maretabeachhouse.com**).

After a last cove, the RV destination finally comes into sight

SAGRES

Sagres fortress

Sagres is a lovely laidback bay with a gorgeous beach. A place where you can easily spend a couple of days winding down from the Rota Vicentina trek and reflecting on the marvellous landscapes and encounters en route.

Sagres once boasted a famous school of navigation set up by Henry the Navigator, helping to launch Portugal's Age of Discovery, and the country's great 15th-century explorers Vasco da Gama, Cabral and Magellan spent time preparing here. While nothing is left of the school, it's definitely worth finding time to visit the vast *fortaleza* (fortress) on the nearby Ponta de Sagres headland to the southwest; it was extensively restored in the wake of the devastating 1755 earthquake. Signed pathways lead to a superb clifftop lookout. A second military construction, Fortaleza da Baleeira, stands on the easternmost headland. Despite the bad damage inflicted by Sir Francis Drake in 1587, it is still impressive.

FT EXTENSION TO LAGOS

Walkers who want more can embark on the FT extension that takes three days to reach Lagos. A more difficult route, it heads along the dramatic southern coast with its attractive bays and beaches via Salema and Luz. Details on www.rotavicentina.com

INLAND ROUTE
STAGE 1IR
Odeceixe to São Teotónio

Start	Odeceixe square
Distance	17km
Ascent	350m
Descent	200m
Grade	2
Walking time	4hr 30min
Refreshments	São Miguel
Accommodation	São Teotónio

This wonderfully solitary stage sees few walkers. The ocean is quickly left behind as the HW heads essentially northeast inland via a string of river valleys and wooded ridges that are reached on steep paths. Cork oaks and eucalypts along with scented Mediterranean shrubs and flowers are the flavour of the day. The central section follows the Ribeira Cerrado valley which is subject to flooding in rainy periods – if necessary take the wet-weather variant, but be aware it is not waymarked.

From the square at **Odeceixe** you need the red/white waymarks leading down Rua do Rio then R out to the main road and bridge over the Seixe. Don't cross it but keep straight ahead past the bus stop and onto the quiet road parallel to the river. Further along it's unsurfaced and shady. Where it bears S you're pointed L for a footbridge over a stream and out to a lane. A sharp L (N) leads on to another bridge followed by a short uphill stretch to the road at **São Miguel**. (Refreshments are on hand with a signed 100-metre detour L.)

The R fork quickly leaves the village and passes a camping ground for a plod on a minor road NE accompanied by occasional farms and marshy zones thick with clumps of yellow flags, close to the Ribeira Seca.

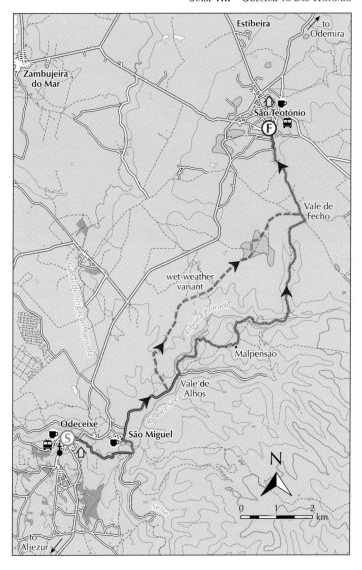

An old farmhouse gradually being overcome by plants

After the wet-weather variant branches L (proceeding gently uphill to rejoin the main route near Vale de Fecho), the main route comes to **Vale de Alhos (1hr 20min)**, a scatter of houses among trees. Here the HW finally leaves the tarmac, forking L (N). It follows the **Ribeira Cerrado** on a stony shady lane which can get waterlogged. ◀ Shortly after a house and a rustic WC you veer R (E) for a stiff climb with vast views over eucalypt plantations. The reward is the panoramic 189m knoll **Malpensao**.

Birdsong and cork oak trees are widespread.

Wide forestry lanes lead N and downhill once more through cool eucalypt wood where stepping stones cross a stream. Further along this left bank, at a pronounced fork in the valley, the way veers L (N). The ensuing extended leisurely stretch concludes with a gentle climb through a sea of rock roses and out to cattle grazing near a farm in **Vale de Fecho**.

Go L on the dirt road to where the wet-weather variant joins up and onto a sandy lane past a boggy pond and power poles, concrete stepping stones helping over wet patches. There are virtually no waymarks on this section, but just go straight ahead, reassured by the occasional stone cairn. The way narrows to a rough sunken path down to a minor ford where a good lane through rural properties takes over, joining a road on the town outskirts. You're pointed through the streets to conclude at the cafés in the inviting central square of **São Teotónio (3hr 10min).** ▸

The spread-out town was named after Portugal's first saint and in spring it is alive with house martins which · nest in the church eaves and tower.

> Sleep at Hotel São Teotonio (tel 283 958406) a 5min walk N. Shops, restaurants, Rede Expressos and Rodoviário buses to Cercal do Alentejo and Odeceixe.

Stage 1R concludes at São Teotónio

STAGE 21R
São Teotónio to Odemira

Start	São Teotónio square
Distance	19km
Ascent	150m
Descent	300m
Grade	1
Walking time	5hr
Refreshments	None en route
Accommodation	Odemira

A relaxing, straightforward stage rambling through undulating farmland and Mediterranean woods and along the cool valleys of the São Teotónio and Mira rivers. Masses of wildflowers will delight spring walkers, as will the pleasant well-served town of Odemira with its sights.

Leave the main square of **São Teotónio** and the church, following the red/white markers past the rows of typical low white houses and E across the river. After orchards is the main road where you fork R through the hamlet of **Quintas**. Not far uphill a sign points you L onto a dirt road through open peaceful farmland with unusual concentrations of scented camomile flowers. A veer L (N) passes through eucalypt plantations before descending gently to cross a concrete bridge over an irrigation channel.

Further on at a derelict house you fork L on a **bridge** in Vale de Linhores, continuing along the shady left bank to a **picnic area**. Farmhouses are dotted here and there. The river is crossed again – stepping stones this time and not far on it's L over a **vehicle bridge**. A lane continues along the pleasant valley of the **Ribeira São Teotónio** with fields and shady trees, to a road (**2hr 30min**), the **halfway mark**.

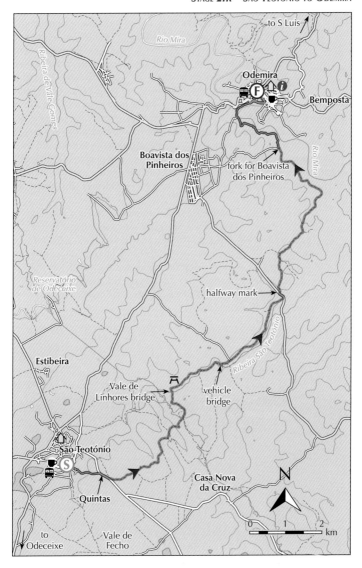

Turn L onto the road and soon take a lane branching R up flower-studded slopes before a gentle descent into the verdant realms of the mighty Rio Mira where huge trees shade the leisurely way. After climbing over a rise through farmland the next landmark is a **fork** (L for Boavista dos Pinheiros – ignore). Tarmac soon leads past the first buildings on the outskirts of Odemira. Up at the main road it's R downhill. (Around the corner by all means shortcut L via the modern footbridge that comes into sight.) A bright red road bridge crosses the Mira then you branch sharp L, quickly dropping to the delightful riverside path that concludes at a roundabout with a gigantic metal tree sculpture in **Odemira (2hr 30min)**. ◄

The charming old part of the town is uphill, as is a worthwhile miradouro *(lookout). The town's name aptly derives from the Arabic for river.*

Odemira lies 30km inland from the coast, however the formerly navigable river, which flows into the ocean at Vila Nova de Milfonte, is still subject to the tides even this far up. Its other claims to fame are a chocolate factory and the HQ of both the marvellous Parque Natural do Sudoeste Alentejano e Costa Vicentina and the Rota Vicentina organisation, no less!

Lush countryside after Quintas

Tourist office (tel 283 320986 turismo.cm-odemira.pt), shops, restaurants and buses – Rede Expressos to Lisbon and Rodoviária to Cacém and elsewhere. Sleep at centrally located Residencial Rita (tel 283 322531 **www.residencial-rita.com**).

The red bridge over the Rio Mira leading into Odemira

STAGE 3IR
Odemira to São Luis

Start	Odemira roundabout
Distance	25km
Ascent	410m
Descent	250m
Grade	2
Walking time	6hr 30min
Refreshments	Nothing en route
Accommodation	São Luis

This long day starts out through farmland quickly followed by a rather dreary crossing through extensively logged eucalypt plantations that have dramatically transformed the landscape. Battlefields come to mind. Thankfully this is followed by a fascinating detour (included in the total stage distance and timing) to the lovely rock pools at Pego das Pias. Thereafter it's a ramble along a lush green river valley before a climb through cereal fields to a sleepy agricultural village for a well-deserved rest.

No difficulties are encountered en route, although due to the length it deserves a Grade 2 rating. Start out as early as possible so you have plenty of time to enjoy this pleasant stage.

From the roundabout with the tree sculpture at **Odemira** turn N following the sign for 'Centro de Saúde Urgências' (health centre). HW waymarking soon appears, as does a sign reassuring you that São Luis is 25km away. Once past the health centre a quiet rural road leads through smallholdings and onto a lane into a valley where the Rio Mira makes a final appearance.

Now you embark on a messy logging track with a stream crossing before an abrupt L to climb steeply over a ridge for a plunge into dense woodland. Follow the waymarks carefully at the many forks. Uphill again an open ridge shows logging devastation as far as the eye can see.

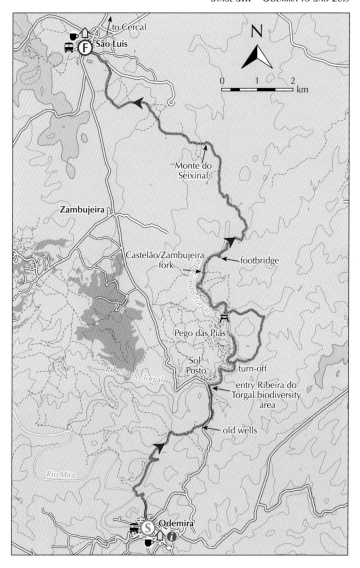

A dirt track continues E, thankfully dropping into a green wooded valley where birdsong is immediately obvious. Two **old wells** precede a road crossing then a clear lane continues through gated farm properties. A stretch N sees you enter the **Ribeira do Torgal biodiversity area** and a welcome shady stroll alongside the gently winding river.

A perfect picnic spot, not to mention a favourite with campers.

At the Pego das Pias **turn-off** (**1hr 45min**) there is a 2km return path to a rocky river gorge with swimming holes. ◀

Back at the turn-off you part ways momentarily with the river to head N up a wooded valley under power lines on a roller-coaster route touching on modest well-spaced farms before returning to the welcome verdant Torgal river valley. A **picnic table** and bridge where the river splits into two branches mark the halfway point (**1hr 30min**).

Small farms are passed en route to Ribeira do Torgal

Not far on you ignore a **fork** L for Castelão and Zambujeira (3.5km away, refreshments) and continue on to a **footbridge** L. Now you bid farewell to the cool river and croaking frogs and embark on a gentle climb in drier terrain with cork oaks and rock roses. A final

Typical church at São Luis

stream crossing precedes marvellous open landscapes with wide-reaching views over cereal fields and livestock farms. Mostly NW, the way leads through a clutch of conifers then past the property **Monte do Seixinal**. Over a rise with a cork oak plantation the white houses of São Luis finally appear on the horizon – but like a mirage they never seem to get any closer!

At last you reach well-kept cottages and join a road L for the final 1km to the crossroads at **São Luis (3hr 15min)**.

Shops, restaurants and cafés. Rede Expressos buses to Lisbon. Rooms at Alves Olive, perfectly located near the crossroads (tel 936 939654).

STAGE 4lR
São Luis to Cercal do Alentejo

Start	Crossroads at São Luis
Distance	20km
Ascent	410m
Descent	400m
Grade	2
Walking time	5hr
Refreshments	None en route
Accommodation	Cercal do Alentejo

The first part of today's stage mostly takes a marvellous high ridge with vast views to inland plains as well as the Rio Mira and the Atlantic coast. However, there's a downside as once again you're traversing extensive eucalypt plantations that occupy entire mountain and hillsides that resemble terraced open-cut mines due to ongoing logging operations. On the upside it must be said that native regrowth is remarkably quick off the mark, and rock rose shrubs and lavender make a swift appearance. More good news is that the second half of the stage rambles through native woodland and rural landscapes the rest of the way to Cercal do Alentejo, a lively town with decent facilities and amenities.

Note: unless you ardently desire to stand on what is reputedly the highest point of the Rota Vicentina (329m), a 1.5km/20min stretch can be avoided near the start by bypassing the São Domingo lookout – in any case today's route is highly panoramic. A further 20min can be saved by excluding the Rocha de Ágra d'Alte detour later on if needed.

Leave the crossroads at **São Luis** along Rua do Comércio to where you're pointed L past old houses, orchards and pretty cottages. A path then a steep lane lead quickly W up to the **fork** (**30min**) for the out-and-back extension

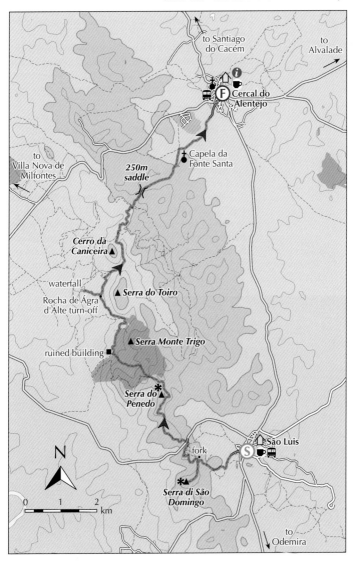

to Santiago
do Cacém

to
Alvalade

Cercal do
Alentejo

F

to
Villa Nova de
Milfontes

Capela da
Fonte Santa

*250m
saddle*

*Cerro da
Caniceira* ▲

waterfall

▲ *Serra do Toiro*

Rocha de Ágra
d'Alte turn-off

▲ *Serra Monte Trigo*

ruined building ■

Serra do ▲
Penedo

São Luis

S

N

fork

*Serra di São
Domingo*

0   1   2
km

to
Odemira

to the superb **Serra di São Domingo** lookout for wide-reaching views.

Back at the fork the way proceeds NW over a rise to cross a road – with care. Then a wide logging track in ascent leads mostly N through terraces of eucalypts past and present, a vast transformed landscape.

From the **ridge** of almost 300m altitude, you admire a lengthy section both up and down the inspiring Atlantic coast along with rolling inland hills, São Luis and the Rio Mira as well as Vila Nova de Milfontes, recognisable for its landmark bridge.

After a stretch at the foot of the **Serra do Penedo** rock outcrop, a drawn-out stony descent NW leaves the ridge. Down at a sizeable clearing it's R (N) past a large **ruined building** and on to traverse a grassed slope and stream. A level dirt road continues on to where eucalypts and logging resume before the **Rocha de Ágra d'Alte turn-off** (**2hr 15min**) a bit over halfway.

At the top of the Rocha de Ágra d'Alte waterfall

A farmhouse on the outskirts of Cercal do Alentejo

For this detour, take the lane that enters Vale Porquinhas for a 10min stroll to a peaceful oasis at the top of a **waterfall** above lush forest. ▶

Back at the turn-off, keep L (NE) and along a minor stream valley followed by a climb through Mediterranean woodland with coastal views. Cork oaks and bracken accompany the track to an atmospheric spot with forlorn buildings and laden fruit trees. Enjoy the last views of the ocean and the Mira as the dirt road winds uphill to a broad **250m saddle**.

Gentle descent leads NE with scented broom, scattered houses and cork oaks. Further down, with the Cercal pulp mill ahead, the RV veers R past a whitewashed **chapel** (Capela da Fonte Santa) and on to welltended orchards and vegetable gardens. The way is surfaced and you're pointed through streets and houses to the main square of **Cercal do Alentejo (2hr 15min)** ringed by inviting cafés.

Unfortunately you can't see the 30m drop without risking a fall over the edge!

The square at Cercal do Alentejo

Tourist office (tel 269 904187 turismo@cm-santiago cacem.pt), Rede Expressos buses to Lisbon, Rodoviária buses to Milfonte and Odemira, shops, restaurants. Stay at the hotel Azul Alentejano (tel 269 949227 **http://azulalentejanohotel.com/**) or take a room at Baú Doce (tel 269 904116 or 964 261055) above the *pastelaria* (cake shop/café) in the main square.

APPENDIX A
Accommodation

Aljezur
Amazigh Hostel
tel 282 997502
www.amazighostel.com

Rooms at Guesthouse A Lareira
tel 282 998440

Almograve
Pousada da Juventude
tel 283 010532
https://pousadasjuventude.pt

Almograve Beach Hostel
tel 963 373635

Arrifana
Arrifana Lounge Guesthouse
tel 282 997496
www.arrifanalounge.com

Hi Arrifana Hostel
tel 282 997455
www.destinationhostels.com

Boutique Guesthouse Releash Aljezur
tel 963 984221
https://releash-aljezur.com/

Carrapateira
Pensao das Dunas
tel 282 973118
www.pensao-das-dunas.pt

Hostel do Mar
tel 960 269668
https://hosteldomar.com

Cercal do Alentejo
Azul Alentejano
tel 269 949227
http://azulalentejanohotel.com/

Baú Doce
tel 269 904116 or 964 261055

4.5km from Cercal do Alentejo:
Herdade da Matinha
tel 933 739245
www.herdadedamatinha.com

En route to Porto Covo
Cabeça da Cabra
tel 966 295432
https://cabecadacabra.com

Moinhos do Paneiro
Moinhos do Paneiro
tel 937 184176
www.moinhosdopaneiro.com

Monte Novo
Barranco da Ponte
tel 282 973223
www.barrancodafonte.pt
(request dinner in advance)

Odeceixe
Hospedaria Firmino Bernardino
tel 282 947362

Odeceixe Hostel
tel 913 919357

Odemira
Residencial Rita
tel 283 322531
www.residencial-rita.com

Pedralva
Aldeia da Pedralva
tel 282 639342
www.aldeiadapedralva.com

Porto Covo
Ahoy Hostel
tel 269 959014
www.ahoyportocovohostel.com

Zé Inacio
tel 269 959136
zeinacio.portocovo@gmail.com

Rogil
Alcatruz Hotel
tel 282 998203
www.hotelalcatruz.com

Sagres
Lighthouse Hostel
tel 282 625341
www.thelighthousehostel.com

Mareta Beach Boutique B&B
tel 282 620040
www.maretabeachhouse.com

Santiago do Cacém
Residencial Covas
tel 269 822675

Hotel Dom Nuno
tel 269 823325
http://hoteldomnuno.com

São Luis
Alves Olive
tel 936 939654

São Teotónio
Hotel São Teotonio
tel 283 958406

near Vale Seco
Casinhas da Aldeia
tel 926 135594/962 284363
https://casinhas-da-aldeia.negocio.site/
fatima.krus@gmail.com

Vila do Bispo
Hotel Mira Sagres
tel 925 408080
www.hotelmirasagres.com

Flor de Esteva
tel 916 868689
https://en.pureaccommodations.com/

Vila Nova de Milfontes
Casa da Adro
tel 917 171811
www.casadoadro.com.pt

Blue Guide rooms
tel 968 780680
blueguidegh@gmail.com or
stayinalentejo@gmail.com

Zambujeira do Mar
Hostel Hakuna Matata
tel 918 470038

Ondazul
tel 283 961450
http://ondazul.zambujeira-do-mar.
hotels-pt.net/it/

APPENDIX B
Useful information

Tourist offices

Almograve
tel 283 647643
https://turismo.cm-odemira.pt

Cercal do Alentejo
tel 269 904187
turismo@cm-santiagocacem.pt

Lisbon
tel 210 312700
www.visitlisboa.com

Odemira
tel 283 320986
https://turismo.cm-odemira.pt

Porto Covo
tel 269 959120
turismo.portocovo@gmail.com

Sagres
tel 282 624873
www.visitalgarve.pt

Santiago do Cacém
tel 269 826696
https://turismo.cm-santiagocacem.pt

Vila Nova de Milfontes
tel 283 996599
https://turismo.cm-odemira.pt

Zambujeira do Mar
tel 283 961144
https://turismo.cm-odemira.pt

Transport

Buses
Rede Expressos (www.rede-expressos.pt) connects Lisbon with Porto Covo, Cercal do Alentejo, Santiago do Cacém, Vila Nova de Milfontes, Almograve, Zambujeira do Mar, Odeceixe, Aljezur, Carrapateira as well as Lagos.

Rodoviária do Alentejo (www.rodalentejo.pt) serves Cercal do Alentejo, Vila Nova de Milfontes, Odemira and others.

EVA Transportes (http://eva-bus.com) does Odeceixe, Aljezur, Vila do Bispo, Cabo de São Vicente, Sagres, Lagos among others.

Trains
The state railway Comboios de Portugal (www.cp.pt) is handy from Lagos via Tunes to Faro or Lisbon.

Taxis
Note: you can always ask your accommodation provider to find you a taxi.

Aljezur: Luís Marreiro
tel 917 574630

Almograve: Isabel Costa
tel 926 131225

Carrapateira: José Pacheco
tel 962 777720

Cercal do Alentejo: Carlos Manuel
Domingos
tel 964 596036

Odeceixe: Sílvia Novais
tel 939 780396

Porto Covo: Aníbal Tomé Pereira
tel 967 678171

Sagres: Rui Pinheiro
tel 964 858517
www.taxi-t.com

Santiago do Cacém: Nuno Carlos
tel 968 959628

Vila Nova de Milfontes: Helder Brás
tel 917 347413

Zambujeira do Mar: Nelson Eliziário
tel 961 230222

Emergencies
General emergencies
tel 112

Forest fires
tel 117

Rota Vicentina
The excellent Rota Vicentina official
website (http://en.rotavicentina.com)
has tons of helpful information as well
as links for booking accommodation
and organising transfers and guided
treks. Their office at Odemira can be
contacted on tel 969 275975.

Transfers and luggage transport
www.vicentinatransfers.pt

Nature Trekks
https://naturetrekks.com

APPENDIX C

Portuguese–English glossary

Greetings and food vocabulary can be found in the Introduction. Other terms found along the way are listed here:

Portugese	English
aberto	open
ajuda/socorro!	help!
alojamento local, hospedaria, quartos, residencial	accommodation, rooms for rent
arriba	cliff
barranco	ravine
bilhete	ticket
castelo	castle
cidade	town
comboios	trains, railway
fechado	closed
fonte	spring
fortaleza	fortress
foz	river mouth
horários	timetable
ida	single (ticket)
ida e volta	return (ticket)
igreja	church

Portugese	English
ilha	island
levada	irrigation channel, aqueduct
miradouro	lookout
moinho	windmill
padaria	bakery
pastelaria	cake shop
paragem	stop (eg bus)
pequeno-almoço	breakfast
perigo!	danger!
ponta	point, headland
pousada de juventude	youth hostel
praia	beach
ribeira, rio	creek, river
rua	road
sande, sandes	sandwich
terminal rodoviário	bus station

DOWNLOAD THE ROUTES
IN GPX FORMAT

All the routes in this guide are available for download from:

www.cicerone.co.uk/1143/GPX

as standard format GPX files. You should be able to load them into most online GPX systems and mobile devices, whether GPS or smartphone. You may need to convert the file into your preferred format using a conversion programme such as gpsvisualizer.com or one of the many other such websites and programmes.

When you follow this link, you will be asked for your email address and where you purchased the guidebook, and have the option to subscribe to the Cicerone e-newsletter.

www.cicerone.co.uk

LISTING OF CICERONE GUIDES

BRITISH ISLES CHALLENGES,
COLLECTIONS AND ACTIVITIES
Great Walks on the England
    Coast Path
Map and Compass
The Big Rounds
The Book of the Bivvy
The Book of the Bothy
The Mountains of England and Wales:
    Vol 1 Wales
    Vol 2 England
The National Trails
Walking the End to End Trail

SHORT WALKS SERIES
Short Walks Hadrian's Wall
Short Walks in the Lake District:
    Keswick, Borrowdale and
    Buttermere
Short Walks in the Lake District:
    Windermere Ambleside and
    Grasmere
Short Walks in the Lake District:
    Coniston and Langdale
Short Walks in Arnside and Silverdale
Short Walks in Nidderdale
Short Walks in Northumberland:
    Wooler, Rothbury, Alnwick and
    the coast
Short Walks on the Malvern Hills
Short Walks in Cornwall:
    Falmouth and the Lizard
Short Walks in Cornwall:
    Land's End and Penzance
Short Walks in the South Downs:
    Brighton, Eastbourne and Arundel
Short Walks in the Surrey Hills
Short Walks Winchester
Short Walks in Pembrokeshire:
    Tenby and the south
Short Walks on the Isle of Mull
Short Walks on the Orkney Islands

SCOTLAND
Ben Nevis and Glen Coe
Cycling in the Hebrides
Cycling the North Coast 500
Great Mountain Days in Scotland
Mountain Biking in Southern and
    Central Scotland
Mountain Biking in West and North
    West Scotland
Not the West Highland Way
Scotland
Scotland's Best Small Mountains
Scotland's Mountain Ridges
Scottish Wild Country Backpacking
Short Walks in Dumfries and
    Galloway
Skye's Cuillin Ridge Traverse
The Borders Abbeys Way
The Great Glen Way

The Great Glen Way Map Booklet
The Hebridean Way
The Hebrides
The Isle of Mull
The Isle of Skye
The Skye Trail
The Southern Upland Way
The West Highland Way
West Highland Way Map Booklet
Walking Ben Lawers, Rannoch
    and Atholl
Walking in the Cairngorms
Walking in the Pentland Hills
Walking in the Scottish Borders
Walking in the Southern Uplands
Walking in Torridon, Fisherfield,
    Fannichs and An Teallach
Walking Loch Lomond and the
    Trossachs
Walking on Arran
Walking on Harris and Lewis
Walking on Jura, Islay and Colonsay
Walking on Rum and the Small Isles
Walking on the Orkney and
    Shetland Isles
Walking on Uist and Barra
Walking the Cape Wrath Trail
Walking the Corbetts
    Vol 1 South of the Great Glen
    Vol 2 North of the Great Glen
Walking the Galloway Hills
Walking the John o' Groats Trail
Walking the Munros
    Vol 1 — Southern, Central and
    Western Highlands
    Vol 2 — Northern Highlands and
    the Cairngorms
Winter Climbs in the Cairngorms
Winter Climbs: Ben Nevis and
    Glen Coe

NORTHERN ENGLAND ROUTES
Cycling the Reivers Route
Cycling the Way of the Roses
Hadrian's Cycleway
Hadrian's Wall Path
Hadrian's Wall Path Map Booklet
Pennine Way Map Booklet
The Coast to Coast Cycle Route
The Coast to Coast Walk
The Coast to Coast Map Booklet
The Pennine Way
Walking the Dales Way
The Dales Way Map Booklet

LAKE DISTRICT
Bikepacking in the Lake District
Cycling in the Lake District
Great Mountain Days in the
    Lake District
Joss Naylor's Lakes, Meres and
    Waters of the Lake District

Lake District Winter Climbs
Lake District:
    High Level and Fell Walks
    Low Level and Lake Walks
Mountain Biking in the
    Lake District
Outdoor Adventures with Children
    — Lake District
Scrambles in the Lake District —
    North
    South
Trail and Fell Running in the
    Lake District
Walking The Cumbria Way
Walking the Lake District Fells —
    Borrowdale
    Buttermere
    Coniston
    Keswick
    Langdale
    Mardale and the Far East
    Patterdale
    Wasdale
Walking the Tour of the Lake District

NORTH—WEST ENGLAND AND
THE ISLE OF MAN
Cycling the Pennine Bridleway
Isle of Man Coastal Path
The Lancashire Cycleway
The Lune Valley and Howgills
Walking in Cumbria's Eden Valley
Walking in Lancashire
Walking in the Forest of Bowland
    and Pendle
Walking on the Isle of Man
Walking on the West Pennine Moors
Walking the Ribble Way
Walks in Silverdale and Arnside

NORTH—EAST ENGLAND,
YORKSHIRE DALES AND
PENNINES
Cycling in the Yorkshire Dales
Great Mountain Days in the Pennines
Mountain Biking in the Yorkshire
    Dales
The Cleveland Way and the
    Yorkshire Wolds Way
The Cleveland Way Map Booklet
The North York Moors
Trail and Fell Running in the
    Yorkshire Dales
Walking in County Durham
Walking in Northumberland
Walking in the North Pennines
Walking in the Yorkshire Dales:
    North and East
    South and West
Walking St Cuthbert's Way
Walking St Oswald's Way and
    Northumberland Coast Path

DERBYSHIRE, PEAK DISTRICT AND MIDLANDS

Cycling in the Peak District
Dark Peak Walks
Scrambles in the Dark Peak
Walking in Derbyshire
Walking in the Peak District — White Peak East
Walking in the Peak District — White Peak West

WALES AND WELSH BORDERS

Cycle Touring in Wales
Cycling Lon Las Cymru
Great Mountain Days in Snowdonia
Hillwalking in Shropshire
Mountain Walking in Snowdonia
Offa's Dyke Path
Offa's Dyke Map Booklet
Scrambles in Snowdonia
Snowdonia: 30 Low-level and Easy Walks
— North
— South
The Cambrian Way
The Pembrokeshire Coast Path
Pembrokeshire Coast Path Map Booklet
The Snowdonia Way
The Wye Valley Walk
Walking Glyndwr's Way
Walking in Carmarthenshire
Walking in Pembrokeshire
Walking in the Brecon Beacons
Walking in the Forest of Dean
Walking in the Wye Valley
Walking on Gower
Walking the Severn Way
Walking the Shropshire Way
Walking the Wales Coast Path

SOUTHERN ENGLAND

20 Classic Sportive Rides in South East England
20 Classic Sportive Rides in South West England
Cycling in the Cotswolds
Mountain Biking on the North Downs
Mountain Biking on the South Downs
Suffolk Coast and Heath Walks
The Cotswold Way
The Cotswold Way Map Booklet
The Kennet and Avon Canal
The Lea Valley Walk
The North Downs Way
North Downs Way Map Booklet
The Peddars Way and Norfolk Coast Path
The Pilgrims' Way
The Ridgeway National Trail
The Ridgeway Map Booklet
The South Downs Way
The South Downs Way Map Booklet
The Thames Path
The Thames Path Map Booklet
The Two Moors Way

Two Moors Way Map Booklet
Walking Hampshire's Test Way
Walking in Cornwall
Walking in Essex
Walking in Kent
Walking in London
Walking in Norfolk
Walking in the Chilterns
Walking in the Cotswolds
Walking in the Isles of Scilly
Walking in the New Forest
Walking in the North Wessex Downs
Walking on Dartmoor
Walking on Guernsey
Walking on Jersey
Walking on the Isle of Wight
Walking the Dartmoor Way
Walking the Jurassic Coast
Walking the Sarsen Way
Walking the South West Coast Path
South West Coast Path Map Booklet
— Vol 1: Minehead to St Ives
— Vol 2: St Ives to Plymouth
— Vol 3: Plymouth to Poole
Walks in the South Downs National Park
Cycling Land's End to John o' Groats

ALPS CROSS—BORDER ROUTES

100 Hut Walks in the Alps
Alpine Ski Mountaineering Vol 1 — Western Alps
The Karnischer Hohenweg
The Tour of the Bernina
Trail Running — Chamonix and the Mont Blanc region
Trekking Chamonix to Zermatt
Trekking in the Alps
Trekking in the Silvretta and Ratikon Alps
Trekking Munich to Venice
Trekking the Tour du Mont Blanc
Tour du Mont Blanc Map Booklet
Walking in the Alps

FRANCE, BELGIUM, AND LUXEMBOURG

Camino de Santiago — Via Podiensis
Chamonix Mountain Adventures
Cycle Touring in France
Cycling London to Paris
Cycling the Canal de la Garonne
Cycling the Canal du Midi
Mont Blanc Walks
Mountain Adventures in the Maurienne
Short Treks on Corsica
The GR5 Trail
The GR5 Trail — Vosges and Jura
Benelux and Lorraine
The Grand Traverse of the Massif Central
The Moselle Cycle Route
Trekking in the Vanoise

Trekking the Cathar Way
Trekking the GR10
Trekking the GR20 Corsica
Trekking the Robert Louis Stevenson Trail
Via Ferratas of the French Alps
Walking in Provence — East
Walking in Provence — West
Walking in the Auvergne
Walking in the Brianconnais
Walking in the Dordogne
Walking in the Haute Savoie: North
Walking in the Haute Savoie: South
Walking on Corsica
Walking the Brittany Coast Path
Walking in the Ardennes

PYRENEES AND FRANCE/SPAIN CROSS—BORDER ROUTES

Shorter Treks in the Pyrenees
The Pyrenean Haute Route
The Pyrenees
Trekking the Cami dels Bons Homes
Trekking the GR11 Trail
Walks and Climbs in the Pyrenees

SPAIN AND PORTUGAL

Camino de Santiago: Camino Frances
Costa Blanca Mountain Adventures
Cycling the Camino de Santiago
Mountain Walking in Mallorca
Mountain Walking in Southern Catalunya
Spain's Sendero Historico: The GR1
The Andalucian Coast to Coast Walk
The Camino del Norte and Camino Primitivo
The Camino Ingles and Ruta do Mar
The Mountains Around Nerja
The Sierras of Extremadura
Trekking in Mallorca
Trekking in the Canary Islands
Trekking the GR7 in Andalucia
Walking and Trekking in the Sierra Nevada
Walking in Andalucia
Walking in Catalunya — Barcelona
Girona Pyrenees
Walking in the Picos de Europa
Walking La Via de la Plata and Camino Sanabres
Walking on Gran Canaria
Walking on La Gomera and El Hierro
Walking on La Palma
Walking on Lanzarote and Fuerteventura
Walking on Tenerife
Walking on the Costa Blanca
Walking the Camino dos Faros
Portugal's Rota Vicentina
The Camino Portugues
Walking in Portugal
Walking in the Algarve

For full information on all our
guides, books and eBooks,
visit our website:
www.cicerone.co.uk